TRAGEDY OF BENAZIR BHUTTO 1953-2007

TRAGEDY OF BENAZIR BHUTTO 1953-2007

Dr. M. Ahmed

SUMIT ENTERPRISES
DELHI 110 002

First Published 2008

ISBN 978-81-8420-091-1

Published by:

SUMIT ENTERPRISES
4649B/21, Ansari Road, Darya Ganj
New Delhi 110002
Phones: 011-23279353
Mob. 9810217567
E-mail: sumit_enterprises2007@yahoo.co.in

PRINTED IN INDIA

Published by Sri Lokesh Gupta for Sumit Enterprises, New Delhi-110002, Typeset by Rajesh Data Services, Printed at

Preface

"Who lives if the country dies and
who dies if the country lives".

Benazir lived and died for her country. She sacrificed her life for a democratic and free life of her country from the undemocratic forces. She becomes one of the bravest women of Asia nay the world. In her death for the cause of her nation she is immortalised and shall live for ever for generations to come. Pakistan has lost a great political leader and the world, one of the ambitious and courageous woman.

Limited aim of this book is to pay tribute to this bold woman and in the process to describe how and why of her career and achievements in her life and in the history of her country.

This book was not possible with out the prompt media, excellent journalism and internet services. We therefore pay our greatful and respectful acknowledgements to them.

Hates off to the equally prompt and expeditious Publication of this book by my publisher who conceived and delivered it as his heart-fell humble tribute to the great daughter of tragedy.

AUTHOR

Contents

1

Introduction

To understand Benazir Bhutto's life and position, we must know about the country she governs. Pakistan, on the Arabian Sea, is bordered by Iran, Afghanistan, the Soviet Union, the People's Republic of China, and India. Pakistan's climate ranges from semi-arid to desert and its elevation goes from sea level along the Arabian Sea to 20,000 feet above sea level in the northern mountains. The mountains of Pakistan are the northern reaches of the Himalayas.

Agriculture is extremely important to Pakistan. The waters of the Indus River, which runs through the center of the country, provide the means to irrigate the crops. Within the borders of Pakistan are the remains of one of the earliest civilizations, yet Pakistan, as a country did not exist until 1947. To understand the modern country, some knowledge of the ancient history of the area is important. Along the banks of the Indus are the ruins of the Harappan culture. This culture flourished five thousand years ago, and archaeologists have determined from the ruins that this culture had a high degree of sophistication, In fact, the residents of Harappan cities like Mohenjo-Daro in Sindh Province probably had better sanitation and a higher standard of living than many of the residents of Pakistan today.

Over the next few thousand years, the area that is now Pakistan was carved up, fought over, and marched through by a variety of peoples and empires. Alexander the Great marched eastward as far as the Indus. The Kushan Empire, the Mauryan Empire, and the Imperial Guptas all held sway in Pakistan at one time. Hinduism, Buddhism, Brahmanism, and Tantricism were just some of the religions practiced in the area. It was not until the seventh and eighth centuries A.D. that a unifying force returned to the area.

In the early seventh century, the Prophet Muhammad put forth the teachings that would later be called the religion of Islam. Modern Islam is based on the Quran, the holy book of the Muslims, which contains the revelations of Allah (God) to Muhammad. The Muslims believe that there is only one God (Allah), who spoke to the people through his messenger Muhammad. Muslims, people who believe in Islam, are supposed to pray five times a day facing the holy city of Mecca, where Muhammad was born, which is in Saudi Arabia. Muslims are expected to visit Mecca once in their lifetime.

Within the historically brief time of two hundred years, the influence of Islam spread westward across northern Africa into Spain and eastward into central Asia. The first incursion into what is today Pakistan occurred in 711, when an Arab expedition invaded Baluchistan and Sind.

Over the next few hundred years, the influence of Islam grew. Muslim teachers spread among the people of the region and paved the way for the Islamic conquest of the subcontinent by Muslims from the Middle East beginning around the year 1000. By 1300 almost all of the subcontinent was under the control of Muslim rulers. Non-Muslims, who were willing to pay the jizya, or protection tax, were permitted to practice their own religions. Throughout the subcontinent, Muslims, Hindus, and Buddhists coexisted in a dynamic culture that experienced a period of renaissance in the arts and literature.

Except for the sack of Delhi in 1398 by Tamerlane, the

Muslim leaders protected the subcontinent from the Mongol hordes that were conquering much of the rest of the civilized world. However, by the sixteenth century the subcontinent had become so fragmented that the Muslim leaders finally succumbed to invasion from the north.

In 1526, after the first Battle of Panipat, Babur of Fergana controlled the area of the Sultanate of Delhi. Babur and his successors led what is called the Mughal (or Mogul) Empire. During the reign of the Mughal Empire, the subcontinent flourished. But by 1707, the Mughal sun had begun to set.

At about the same time, a new player on the subcontinent appeared. The Europeans, first in the personage of the Portuguese sailor Vasco da Gama, landed on the Malabar coast in 1498. The Portuguese wrested control of the Indian Ocean from the Arabs, and the floodgates of trade were thrown open. Not to be outdone, other European countries—England, France, and Holland—joined the rush to establish trading stations in the Indies. The Dutch East India Company concentrated mainly on the spice trade in what is now Indonesia. The East India Company (British) traded with India as did the French East India Company.

The various regional leaders in India negotiated with the French, English, Dutch, and Portuguese traders with all sides vying for the upper hand on the subcontinent. Robert Clive, in 1757, won the decisive victory for the British East India Company at Plassey when he defeated the Nawab of Bengal, Siraj ud Daula. Clive then defeated the Mughal Emperor Shah Alam at the Battle of Buxar in 1764, and for nearly two hundred years the subcontinent labored under the Union Jack, the flag of Great Britain.

Unlike North and South America, which had a small native population that the Europeans were able to subdue and supplant, the subcontinent was much more of a business venture for the British. The East India Company was interested in only one thing from the colony of India: profit.

To ensure a continuing flow of goods out of India and to increase the markets for the factories of England, the

East India Company continued to expand British influence on the subcontinent. Campaign after campaign was fought to acquire more territory. Throughout the first half of the nineteenth century, the company fought for and won additional lands on the subcontinent.

The year 1857 marks a turning point in British-Indian relations. The Indian Mutiny, or Sepoy Rebellion, a revolt by native soldiers in the employ of the East India Company, forced Britain to reevaluate its position in India. The revolt started over the issuing of new Enfield rifles to the troops. These new guns used a cartridge that had to be bitten open before it was inserted into the breech of the rifle. These cartridges were greased, and it was the grease that caused the problem. The Muslim soldiers believed that the grease used was from pig fat; the Hindu soldiers believed it was grease made from cow fat. In either case the thought of inserting the by-product of a forbidden food in one's mouth set off the rebellion.

After the Sepoy Rebellion, England replaced the East India Company with a colonial government directly responsible to Britain's Queen. By unifying India into one political entity, the British planted the seed that would eventually grow into nationalism for India and Pakistan. The Indian National Congress was set up in 1895 to give Indians a forum for expressing their concerns about the governing of the subcontinent.

As the twentieth century began, the feelings of nationalism intensified. The India Councils Act of 1909 gave the people of the subcontinent limited participation in the governing of India. As the British bureaucracy grew, so did the role of Indians in running it. The closer India grew toward autonomy, the more apparent the problems of the minorities became. The largest minority within the territory of British India was the Muslims.

In 1906 the Muslim League was founded to champion the causes of Muslims in India. Over the next forty years the Muslim minority of India, which was most concentrated in the northwestern and the northeastern corners of India, saw themselves more as a community joined by their religion than as a part of the heterogeneous country of India. Out of this feeling grew the idea for a separate Muslim state. In the early 1930s the idea that there should be a separate Muslim state was put forth by Mohammad Iqbal, a Muslim poet. In 1933 a group of Muslim students from the subcontinent who were studying at Cambridge University in England published a pamphlet entitled Now or Never. In the pamphlet they supported the idea of a separate Muslim state. They proposed to call this Muslim state Pakistan, meaning the land of the Paks, the spiritually pure. The pamphlet also made an anagram of the word "Pakistan" stating that the letters came from the names of the Muslim regions of the area: Punjab, Afghana (Northwest Frontier Province), Kashmir, Iran, Sind, Turkharistan, Afghanistan, Baluchistan.

During this time, two organizations led the independence movement. Mohandas K. Gandhi led the Indian National Congress and Mohammad Ali Jinnah led the All-India Muslim League. At times the two groups cooperated in trying to escape the yoke of British colonialism. Often, however, they were in opposition to each other, especially as the movement for a separate Islamic state grew.

Gandhi's congress continued to push for a unified India. The conflict began to grow violent as rioting broke out between Muslims and Hindus. It is interesting to note that in the areas that eventually became East and West Pakistan, where the Muslims held the majority, the league was much less powerful. The greatest problems arose where the minority Muslims feared that they would be discriminated against by the Hindu majority.

By 1945 the end of World War II in Europe and a victory for the Labour Party in England, among other factors, helped make independence for the subcontinent a foregone conclusion. The communal violence between Hindus and Muslims brought the subcontinent to the brink of civil war.

The English Lord Louis Mountbatten was sent to India in February 1947 as Viceroy, with instructions from London to transfer power to the Indian people by June of 1948.

Mountbatten assessed the situation and the positions of the factions involved and saw the need to act as quickly as possible. He astutely realized that the Hindu congress would accept partition in exchange for independence. He also saw that Jinnah and the Muslim League would rather take a smaller Pakistan than none at all and the people caught in the middle would learn to live with partition.

On July 14, 1947, the British House of Commons passed the India Independence Act, creating the modern states of Pakistan and India. The summer of 1947 was plagued by drought, floods, and violence, and all sides learned how inadequately prepared they were for independence.

The Nation of Pakistan

On August 7, 1947, Mohammad Ali Jinnah flew from Delhi to Karachi to become the first Governor-General of Pakistan. When Pakistan officially came into existence one week later on August 14, 1947, the problems that Jinnah faced must have seemed nearly insurmountable. He was the head of a country that the day before had not existed. This country was divided into two parts separated by 1600 kilometers (1000 miles). Within a few months, eight million Hindus and Sikhs had left Pakistan, primarily from the Punjab, and six million Muslims had moved to Pakistan from India. In the process 250,000 people died. The Muslim immigrants in Pakistan became known as the muhajirs. Within the borders of the newly created country of Pakistan was a variety of ethnic and linguistic groups that have yet to meld together.

Jinnah became the head of a country that had no national identity, no national economy, and no national bureaucracy. Pakistan had lost much of its middle class. It faced the problem of dealing with six million muhajirs, many of whom moved into the few urban areas of West Pakistan. It is estimated that the muhajir population of Karachi and the other West Pakistan cities reached as high as 46 percent in 1951.

Possibly the greatest problem facing Jinnah and Pakistan was the lack of experience in self-government. It had been almost five thousand years since the area of West Pakistan had been an autonomous region. East Pakistan—1,000 miles away across a now hostile India would have been nearly ungovernable for even the most experienced and efficient.

The newly formed government of Pakistan depended on the British viceregal model with Jinnah as the governor-general. This too created problems in Pakistan as Benazir Bhutto attempted to continue the democratic reforms begun by her father. Jinnah set the precedent for dictatorial rule that opened the door for the succession of military leaders that followed. Of the forty-odd years that Pakistan has existed, the military has ruled for thirty-two years.

Jinnah's term as governor-general was short-lived. After only thirteen months in office, on September 11, 1948, Jinnah died. His positions were divided among his successors, but the real power of the government fell to Jinnah's right-hand man, Liaquat Ali Khan, who became prime minister.

Liaquat attempted to lead Pakistan toward democracy. His experience as a lawyer under British rule in India gave him the background he needed to understand and strive for parliamentary democracy for Pakistan. Liaquat's efforts might have paved the way for democracy in Pakistan had he not been assassinated in October 1951.

The assassination of Liaquat opened the door to the succession of military leaders that followed. Ghulam Mohammad assumed the position of governor-general and formed an alliance of the military and the landed families of the Punjab. This alliance brought the power of the military to the fore and then weakened and eventually eliminated the powers of the prime minister. As these internal power struggles continued, the problems of a divided country grew. As early as the Second Constituent Congress in 1955, the issue of autonomy for East Pakistan was raised.

Ghulam Mohammad died in August 1955. He was succeeded by General Iskander Mirza, whose rule was marked by turmoil among the various factions within the country. Groups of Muslims argued over what role the religion of Islam should play in the governing of the new country. Mirza alienated the different regions by trying to force the country to become One Unit, as outlined in the 1956 constitution. In 1958 Mirza was forced to invoke martial law when the Khan of Kalat declared independence for Baluchistan, a province in the newly formed Pakistan. The already strained relations between East and West Pakistan were worsened by the assassination of Dr. Kahn Sahib, the chief minister of West Pakistan. On October 27, 1958, President Mirza was sent into exile in Britain by the leading generals of the army.

General Mohammad Ayub Khan became Pakistan's new leader. With the constitution suspended, Ayub was clearly a military dictator. However, he used his power to enact a series of reforms. The rule of Ayub Khan is marked by three basic areas of action. First, Ayub suppressed any possible opposition within or outside the government. Secondly, he put forth a number of reforms ranging from the Muslim Family Laws Ordinance which helped establish some basic rights for women, to major land reforms which put a limit on the amount of land one person could own. Thirdly, he instituted a program of Basic Democracies that were intended to introduce democracy gradually into the country.

It was Ayub's theory that the people could not be ruled democratically until they understood how democracy worked and how they could participate in it. His Basic Democracies program involved setting up a multitiered system starting with a union council. Each council, representing about ten thousand people, worked up to larger councils at higher levels. Ayub felt that the Basic Democracies program would educate the people in self-government. This would help create an arena in which the next generation of politicians could develop. Despite its overtly paternalistic approach, the Basic Democracies offered real hope for bringing democracy to Pakistan. The program was doomed almost from the beginning, however. Factionalism within Pakistan seemed stronger than even the most powerful dictator.

In 1965 Ayub found himself embroiled in a border war with India. The failure of the Ayub government to gain stated objectives in the dispute either militarily or at the bargaining table touched off domestic violence throughout Pakistan. In Lahore and Karachi, angry mobs burned the United States Information Service libraries. By February 1966 the opposition had become so intense that Ayub called for a national conference of political leaders to take place in Lahore. Of the seven hundred delegates present, only twenty-one were from East Pakistan, the more heavily populated part of the country.

The independence sentiments first voiced in 1954 by the East Pakistanis were becoming louder and better organized. The East Pakistani position, under the leadership of Sheikh Mujibur Rahman, kept the conference from proceeding on its stated goals of setting national objectives and issues. Because of the ineffectiveness of the congress to make any progress, among other reasons, Foreign Minister Zulfikar Ali Bhutto resigned and became a leader of the opposition. In late 1967, Bhutto formed a new political party, the Pakistan People's Party. By the early months of 1969, Ayub had lost control of the country. Mob rule was rampant, especially in East Pakistan. The situation was further complicated by Ayub becoming seriously ill. On March 25, 1969, General Agha Mohammad Yahya Khan assumed power and Ayub resigned.

On taking charge of the country, Yahya suspended the Constitution of 1962 and became the Chief Martial Law Administrator. In an attempt to hold the country together, Yahya promised elections. After several delays and postponements the first direct elections in the brief history of Pakistan took place. They were held on December 7, 1970 in most of the country and on January 17, 1971 in some parts of East Pakistan. The Awami League, representing the East Pakistani independence movement, won 167 out of 169 seats allotted to East Pakistan. Bhutto's Pakistan People's Party won a majority in West Pakistan.

2

The Formative Years

Benazir Bhutto was born at Pinto Hospital in Karachi, Pakistan, on June 21, 1953. Her mother, the former Nusrat Ispahani, is the daughter of an Iranian businessman. Her father, Zulfikar Ali Bhutto, was a member of one of Pakistan's wealthiest landowning families, an Oxford educated lawyer, a cabinet minister and ultimately Prime Minister of Pakistan.

Benazir Bhutto was the first child of Zulfikar and Nusrat Bhutto. They had three other children: Mir Murtaza, a son, born in 1954; Sanam, a daughter, born in 1957; and Shah Nawaz, a son, born in 1958.

At birth, Benazir Bhutto's skin was rosy pink, which is unusual among the usually dark-complexioned Pakistanis. Her pink complexion at birth became the basis of her lifelong family nickname: Pinkie. Her given name Benazir means "without comparison." She was named after an aunt who had died while in her early teens. On the day of her birth, her paternal grandmother, Lady Khurshid Bhutto, gave one hundred rupees to a poor man she passed on the street. This is a custom intended to provide a blessing for the newly born child.

Benazir Bhutto's early childhood was spent primarily in Karachi where her father opened his law practice, and at Larkana at the seat of the family estates, Al-Murtaza. Benazir Bhutto grew up with all the trappings of wealth that her family's position near the top of Pakistani society could provide. Servants waited on the family, and one of Benazir Bhutto's first words was supposedly ao, which means enter. She said this to a servant who knocked on the door while she was being toilet-trained.

Although her mother sewed and embroidered dresses for her, as she got older her clothes were more likely to come from Saks Fifth Avenue, an expensive department store in New York City. She had an English governess who taught her western table manners and cared for her and her sister and brothers. English was the language most likely to be spoken by her family, although Persian (her mother's native language), Sindhi (the language of the Sind Province where the Bhutto estates are located), and Urdu (the official language of Pakistan) were also spoken in the Bhutto home.

Both of Benazir Bhutto's parents were Muslims. Zulfikar Ali Bhutto, the rest of the Bhutto family, and most Pakistanis belong to the Sunni branch of Islam. Nusrat Bhutto, like most Iranians, belongs to the Shiite sect. Benazir Bhutto was raised as and is today a Sunni Muslim. Her family, however, was much more progressive in their views than the majority of the people in Pakistan.

This progressive attitude led her parents to provide her with the best education available. A shy but happy child, she started nursery school when she was three, attending the Lady Jenning's Nursery School in Karachi. At age five she was enrolled at the Convent of Jesus and Mary School, run by Irish Catholic nuns. They taught in English and reportedly made no attempt to convert their Muslim students to Catholicism. In addition to her school work, Benazir Bhutto received private tutoring at home in both academic and religious subjects. She had to learn Arabic as part of her religious obligations. The Quran, the Islamic holy book, must be read in Arabic by Muslims.

When Benazir Bhutto was four, her father received his first appointment as a member of Pakistan's delegation to the United Nations, so from that point on, Zulfikar and Nusrat Bhutto were often away from home. When Benazir was eight, she was given the responsibility of keeping the household money while her parents were away. In 1963, when she was ten and her sister Sanam was seven, their governess quit, and they were sent to boarding school.

A branch of the Convent of Jesus and Mary School in Karachi, the boarding school they attended was in Murree, in the northern part of Pakistan in the foothills of the Himalayan mountains; in earlier times it had been the site of a British colonial fort. It was also the location of the Bhutto's summer house. (The elevation in Murree made it a gathering spot for wealthy Pakistanis during the intense summer heat.) At boarding school Benazir Bhutto had to fend for herself. There were no servants, as there were at home, to make her bed or to do the other chores required of her at Murree. She did well under the tutelage of the nuns, although she found it hard to adjust to the strict rules.

Benazir Bhutto was still at Murree two years later when the 1965 Kashmir War broke out between India and Pakistan. Murree is not far from the area that was being fought over and directly on the logical invasion route that India might use. The nuns prepared the students for the possibility of attack, but fortunately the feared invasion never came.

In her early teens Benazir Bhutto returned to the Karachi branch of the Convent of Jesus and Mary school. In 1968, while she was preparing for her 0-level exams, her father was arrested and put in Mianwali Prison, which was known for its horrible conditions. He was later transferred to Sahiwal Prison, where rats shared the cells.

Benazir Bhutto's life was not entirely dedicated to her studies. She and her friends also found time to go to the Sindh Club where they could swim, play squash, and socialize with other young people. Before her father's falling-out with General Ayub, Zulfikar Ali Bhutto would often see to it that Benazir and her siblings would get to meet the various foreign dignitaries visiting Pakistan. This provided her with an early introduction into one aspect of the workings of government.

The 0-Level exams, which cover the last three years of secondary school, were held in December 1968. Due to the unrest in Pakistan at the time, the nuns at the Convent of Joseph and Mary made arrangements for the exams to be administered at the embassy of the Vatican. Benazir Bhutto also took the Scholastic Aptitude Test and an entrance exam for Radcliffe at about the same time. In April of 1969, she was accepted to Radcliffe College, a part of Harvard University in Cambridge, Massachusetts.

Benazir Bhutto at Radcliffe

When Benazir Bhutto arrived at Radcliffe in the fall of 1969, she was only sixteen—two years younger than most of her classmates. She was the first Bhutto woman to attend college in the West. Her mother accompanied her to the United States and stayed in Cambridge for two weeks helping her to get settled. Muslims are required to pray five times a day facing Mecca, their holy city, located in Saudi Arabia. Nusrat Bhutto ascertained Mecca's direction so that her daughter's prayers would be done properly.

Soon after her mother left to return to Pakistan, Benazir Bhutto decided that her traditional Pakistani attire, a shalwar khameez which is a tunic worn with pants, was not the most practical wardrobe for the climate and styles of Cambridge. A trip to the Harvard Coop in Harvard Square provided her with a wardrobe more appropriate for a coed of the time. The Harvard Coop fills the needs of the Harvard community and carries everything from books to toothbrushes and clothes to appliances. Jeans and sweatshirts were the uniform of this generation of college students, and like most college students, Benazir Bhutto seemed to want to fit in. Her hair was already straight, and she let it grow long. Many people pointed out to her that she looked remarkably like the popular folk singer Joan Baez.

In many ways Benazir Bhutto was an enigma to her college friends and acquaintances who came to know her by her family nickname, "Pinkie." On the one hand, she was a typical college student of the time, while on the other hand she continued to observe orthodox Islamic rules. She didn't smoke, drink, take drugs, or eat foods forbidden to Muslims. She did, however, develop a taste for ice cream cones and would often go with her friends to Brigham's in Harvard Square, where she liked to order peppermint stick ice cream with sprinkles. Until she arrived at Radcliffe, she had never answered her own phone or gone anywhere without the family chauffeur to take her. She adhered to some parts of the Muslim dress code by always wearing sweat pants when she played squash since Muslim traditions require women to cover their legs. She observed the Islamic taboo against dancing but would spend hours debating the problems of the world with her friends. She not only talked about the problems; she stood up for her beliefs as well.

Benazir Bhutto was a part of the anti-Vietnam War movement at Harvard. She marched against the Vietnam War on Boston Common and in Washington, D.C. She demonstrated despite the fact that she knew she could have been deported for doing so. Her opposition to the war must have been on political grounds because, when Pakistan fought its civil war in East Pakistan, she was a staunch defender of her country's right to use military force to try and stop the division of the country.

Benazir Bhutto also became interested in the women's movement. It is in part from this interest that she was much later able to see herself as the leader of a country, as a wife, and as a mother at the same time.

When one of her professors, Michael Walzer, criticized Pakistan and its military policies for its role in the civil war in East Pakistan, Benazir Bhutto stood up in class and refuted his statements. Her impassioned defense of her country was the first indication of what a moving and powerful public speaker she would become.

Benazir Bhutto had originally intended to study psychology at Radcliffe but eventually decided to seek a degree in comparative government. It was her plan at this time to enter the diplomatic corps of Pakistan after graduation. This desire was fueled by her father, who would often include her in his official visits to foreign countries when they coincided with her college vacations.

When Benazir Bhutto was a junior at Radcliffe, General Yahya Khan sent Zulfikar Ali Bhutto to the United Nations in New York. He was to try and negotiate a settlement to the Indian military intervention on behalf of the East Pakistani fight for independence. As soon as he learned he was on his way to New York, Zulfikar Ali Bhutto called his daughter and invited her to join him. With the idealism of a college student, Benazir Bhutto expected Pakistan to be vindicated and India to be condemned by the United Nations Security Council. The opposite outcome proved to be a bitter lesson in the politics of power.

For a variety of reasons that had nothing to do with what is just or unjust, the superpowers sided with India, and Bangladesh was created. Zulfikar Ali Bhutto had stormed out of the Security Council in anger, and his daughter had been right behind him. One ironic outcome of Benazir Bhutto's visit to the United Nations was that the woman who would eventually become the prime minister of Pakistan met the man who would later be the president of the United States. George Bush was President Nixon's ambassador to the United Nations and, while visiting Zulfikar Ali Bhutto, was introduced to Benazir Bhutto. Bush remarked at the time that one of his sons was at Harvard with Benazir Bhutto and suggested that, if she needed any assistance, she should look him up.

When her father returned to Pakistan, he was to become the head of the country. As the leader of the largest political party in Pakistan, he was probably the only civilian with sufficient experience in government and enough popular support to lead Pakistan out of its defeat by India and its loss of Bangladesh. On December 20, 1971, Zulfikar Ali Bhutto became president and chief martial law administrator of Pakistan.

As the leader of his country, he continued to include Benazir Bhutto whenever he could, taking her on visits to foreign countries and discussing policy with her. Consciously or unconsciously, he was preparing her to follow in his footsteps.

His first order of business as head of the government was to reach a settlement with India. On June 28, 1972, Benazir Bhutto accompanied her father to Simla, India, where Zulfikar Ali Bhutto and Indian Prime Minister Indira Gandhi met behind closed doors to try and settle their problems. Due in part to the secrecy of their talks, the eye of the media was turned on Benazir Bhutto. She experienced the scrutiny that would continue as she became more and more important in the politics of her country.

While at Radcliffe, Benazir Bhutto also accompanied her father to China and sat in on his meetings with Chairman Mao, which made her liberal, intellectual friends at Harvard green with envy. Benazir Bhutto also visited the Nixon White House when her father was in Washington, D.C., on a state visit.

Benazir Bhutto seemed capable of fitting in wherever she went. She was fond of attending the many athletic events at Harvard. On her frequent visits to the home of Professor John Kenneth Galbraith, the former American ambassador to India, she seemed more like the young woman who would one day lead her country. When she met with other Pakistanis who were part of the Cambridge academic community, she would revert to her traditional clothing and once more seem the aristocrat that she is.

In 1973, Benazir Bhutto graduated cum laude from Radcliffe, which has since been absorbed by Harvard

University. She had learned and experienced much in her four years at Harvard in the turbulent early seventies. Despite the changes she may have gone through, two things remained steadfast: her devotion to Islam and her devotion to Pakistan. The two are intertwined in this woman who was destined for leadership. Pakistan exists as a homeland for the Muslims on the subcontinent, and Benazir Bhutto represents the first generation to be born Pakistani.

Benazir Bhutto at Oxford

Benazir Bhutto entered Lady Margaret Hall at Oxford College in the fall of 1973. Unlike the meek child who had entered Radcliffe four years before, Benazir Bhutto went to Oxford as the daughter of the prime minister of Pakistan and a self-confident young woman. The people of England are generally more aware of the goings-on in their former colonies than the people in the United States. This made Benazir Bhutto more of a celebrity than she had ever been at Radcliffe. Great Britain, with its tenacious continuance of the monarchy, is much more class-conscious than the United States. At Oxford, Benazir Bhutto was more likely to be found among those who were her social and economic equals.

There were no more walks through Harvard Square to go to Brigham's for ice cream. At Oxford she would race off to the newly opened Baskin Robbins in London in the yellow MG convertible that her father had given her. And at Oxford her enjoyment of debating took on a more formalized air as she joined the Oxford Union.

The Oxford Union Debating Society, which was formed in 1823 and is modeled on the British House of Commons, is said to be a training ground for future politicians. Benazir Bhutto joined at her father's request but soon found the Union to her liking. During the many debates she participated in, her powers of oratory, which had only begun to emerge at Radcliffe, blossomed. She also became active in the running of the union. She served on its standing committee and as treasurer. Her first attempt to become president of the Oxford Union Debating Society ended in defeat.

After three years at Oxford she had completed her second Bachelor of Arts degree in philosophy, politics, and economics. She then decided to stay on for another year to study international law and diplomacy and to make another run for the presidency of the union. Her brother, Mir Murtaza Bhutto, joined her at Oxford during her fourth year. In December 1976, after a very energetic campaign, Benazir Bhutto was elected president of the Oxford Union. She served a three-month term which began in January 1977—the first Asian woman to serve as president. Her father had been the first Asian person to hold that office. It is ironic that it would be eleven years before Benazir Bhutto would run for another elected office and that her second political victory would make her prime minister of one hundred million Pakistanis.

Right after graduation, fresh from her success as president of the union, Benazir Bhutto returned to Pakistan to take a job in the office of her father, the prime minister.

3

Zulfikar Ali Bhutto

Zulmar Ali Bhutto was born on January 5, 1928 into one of the rich and powerful landowning families of Sind province. His father, Sir Shah Nawaz Khan Bhutto, had been an active civil servant prior to the creation of Pakistan and had been knighted for his services to the British crown. Zulfikar Ali Bhutto's mother, Lady Khurshid, was from Bombay, India. Born a Hindu, she converted to Islam after her marriage. Sir Shah Nawaz served in many positions within the colonial administration of the subcontinent, primarily in Bombay. Sir Shah Nawaz was also one of the early advocates of the creation of a separate Muslim state on the subcontinent.

Zulfikar Ali Bhutto was raised in this politically active environment while experiencing all the benefits of belonging to one of the elite families of Sind. The Bhuttos can trace their lineage back to antiquity. For 350 years, the family has been based on its land in Sind province. They converted to Islam four hundred years ago and prior to that probably belonged to the aristocratic Rajput caste of Hindu warriors. Sir Shah Nawaz was the youngest son of his particular branch of the family, and the bulk of the land was ruled over by his older brother.

Sir Shah Nawaz was rather progressive and broke with

the traditions of his class when he saw to it that his son, Zulfikar Ali Bhutto, received a modern education. Zulfikar Ali Bhutto was tutored at home until he was nine and was then sent to Cathedral Boys' School in Bombay, where the family was living at the time. On his first attempt at the Senior Cambridge Exam in December 1945, he failed to receive a passing grade. A year later, in December 1946, he passed his Cambridge Exam.

In the fall of 1947, Zulfikar Ali Bhutto enrolled at the University of Southern California and was the first Bhutto to go to school in the West. He transferred to the University of California at Berkeley in January 1949. At Berkeley he majored in political science and graduated with honors in 1950. From California he went to Oxford University in England, where he studied law. He received his Master of Arts in Jurisprudence in 1952 and went to Lincoln's Inn in London to prepare for his bar exams. He was called to the Bar in 1953 but returned to Pakistan where his father had taken ill and his first child awaited him.

In a tradition that was intended to keep the land held by the powerful families, children are often married at an early age to their cousins. Zulfikar Ali Bhutto was no exception. When he was twelve and his cousin Amir was eight, they were married. It was a marriage intended to help maintain the power of the Bhutto clan. After the marriage ceremony, Amir returned to live with her family. In 1951, while Zulfikar Ali Bhutto was home on vacation from Oxford, he met and fell in love with Nusrat Ispahani, the daughter of an Iranian businessman. Zulfikar Ali Bhutto broke with the tradition of marrying within the family and on September 8, 1951, Zulfikar Ali Bhutto and Nusrat were married. Islamic law allows a man to have as many as four wives. Zulfikar Ali Bhutto had asked for and received permission from his first wife, with whom he had never lived, to take a second wife.

Nusrat Bhutto came from a progressive urban family. She and her sisters had not been kept in seclusion, as were girls in many traditional Pakistani families. Nusrat Bhutto and her sisters had been educated and had attended college. They were allowed to drive their own cars and had even served in the National Guard, a paramilitary group made up of women. After marrying, Zulfikar Ali Bhutto and Nusrat Bhutto lived for a time in England. While pregnant, Nusrat Bhutto returned to Pakistan. She lived in seclusion, or purdah, with the other Bhutto women while her husband completed his studies in England.

The first of their four children, Benazir Bhutto, was born at Pinto Hospital in Karachi on June 21, 1953. Zulfikar Ali Bhutto did not meet his new daughter until he returned to Pakistan at the completion of his studies. Benazir Bhutto was three months old when her father finally got to see her.

Now back in Karachi for good, Zulfikar Ali Bhutto opened a law practice and assumed the management of the family lands. Due to his father's illness, the family estates had been neglected. Bhutto put himself to the task of getting things back on track while participating in the social life of Karachi. There is no doubt that he was a well-educated and capable young man, but his position near the top of Pakistani society also played a major part in launching his political career.

Like the British who had ruled them, the landed gentry of Pakistan has a passion for shooting. One of the best shooting preserves in Pakistan is located on the Bhutto family lands. During the first few years after Zulfikar Ali Bhutto returned to Pakistan, he could often be found on the weekends shooting with family and friends. Among the friends of his family who attended these shoots were then President Iskander Mirza and the head of the army, General Ayub Khan. Both men were apparently impressed with the young Berkeley and Oxford-educated lawyer.

President Mirza was determined to utilize the talent of Zulfikar Ali Bhutto within the government. At first Zulfikar Ali Bhutto seemed to be caught up in the machinations of power as Mirza would nominate him for a position and first Prime Minister Choudhury Mohammad Ali and then later Prime Minister Hussain Shaheed Suhrawardy would turn him down.

In September 1957, Zulfikar Ali Bhutto was once again appointed to a position as a member of the United Nations delegation. This time no one objected, and Zulfikar Ali Bhutto, now twenty-nine, was on the road that would eventually lead him to the top of Pakistani politics—and ultimately to his death. At the United Nations, Zulfikar Ali Bhutto gave a speech entitled. "The Definition of Aggression", which was well received. His tenure in New York was cut short when his father died. It took about two months for him to set his father's affairs straight. His next assignment was to attend the United Nations Conference on the Law of the Sea. He impressed people there as well.

On October 7, 1958, Iskander Mirza canceled elections and declared martial law. Just short of three weeks later, on October 27, 1958, General Ayub Khan staged a coup d'etat. President Mirza was exiled, and General Ayub Khan assumed sole command of Pakistan. Although the military was now firmly in control of the country, Ayub wanted to include as many civilians as possible in his new government. Zulfikar Ali Bhutto's social position, talents, education, experience at the United Nations, and friendship with Ayub made him an obvious choice for inclusion in the government.

Zulfikar Ali Bhutto's first appointment under Ayub was as minister of commerce. At age thirty he became the youngest minister in Pakistan's brief history. In 1960, Zulfikar Ali Bhutto gave up his position as minister of commerce, and for the next two years he simultaneously ran four ministries. He became the minister of minority affairs; minister of national reconstruction and information; minister of fuel, power, and natural resources; and minister of Kashmir affairs. When General Ayub Khan instituted a new constitution and reformed his government in 1962, Zulfikar Ali Bhutto was the only original cabinet member to be included in the new government.

Throughout the four years he had served in the first Ayub cabinet, Zulfikar Ali Bhutto had been called on frequently to represent the government of Pakistan as a negotiator with and envoy to a number of foreign countries. He excelled in these situations, so it was not surprising that in the new government he was appointed minister of external affairs, a position comparable to the secretary of state in the United States. Over the next three years he was extremely active in Pakistan's foreign affairs, attending conferences and visiting foreign countries.

During this time, he is credited with reopening relations with Afghanistan, settling boundary disputes with the people's Republic of China, and enhancing Pakistan's image in the world community. When Ayub Khan began his second presidential term, Zulfikar Ali Bhutto retained his position as foreign minister. He was included in Ayub's inner circle as one of his four most trusted advisers.

Although Zulfikar Ali Bhutto was still a member of the right-wing Muslim League, the left-wing politics that he had displayed as a college student in California began to reappear. Ayub Khan was a staunch ally of the United States, while Zulfikar Ali Bhutto saw the U.S. as too domineering and unwilling to give Pakistan the military backing it needed in its struggle against India. Zulfikar Ali Bhutto saw the People's Republic of China, who had its own conflicts with India, as Pakistan's natural ally.

Among other reasons, Zulfikar Ali Bhutto's position as a hard liner against India is part of what eventually caused his falling-out with Ayub Khan. In 1965 the ongoing tension between India and Pakistan once again flared into armed conflict. The undemarcated border between India and Pakistan in the Kashmir was the setting for an increasing number of skirmishes between the troops of both countries. A cease-fire was negotiated in the United Nations Security Council and President Ayub met with Indian Prime Minister Lal Bahadur Shastri at Tashkent in the Soviet Union. A mutual withdrawal of forces was agreed upon. The people of Pakistan were angry because they felt the war had accomplished nothing and had cost too many lives and too much money.

Demonstrations erupted in most of the urban areas of Pakistan. Politicians as well as students demonstrated. A national conference was called, but nothing was accomplished when the East Pakistanis used the conference to push for Bengali independence. Zulfikar Ali Bhutto was among those who saw the Tashkent agreement as a sign of weakness, and he tried to resign from the government. Ayub refused his resignation and, instead, waited until July when he sent Zulfikar Ali Bhutto on a forced sick leave to London and announced Bhutto's resignation.

Zulfikar Ali Bhutto became a vocal opponent of the government of President Ayub. By December 1967, Zulfikar Ali Bhutto had channeled his opposition into forming the Pakistan People's Party. Zulfikar Ali Bhutto's party grew rapidly and soon posed a threat to Ayub's government. On November 13, 1968, Ayub had Zulfikar Ali Bhutto arrested and sent to jail for allegedly causing violent antigovernment demonstrations. Zulfikar Ali Bhutto was released in February 1969. His time in jail enhanced his position as the opposition leader and gave him an aura of martyrdom that fueled his popularity.

The vocal and now often violent opposition to the Ayub government precipitated another coup. In March 1969 General Agha Mohammad Yahya Khan became the next military leader to head the country of Pakistan. Yahya suspended the constitution of 1962 and declared himself chief martial law administrator. Yahya and his generals were caught up in the irresistible forces that were destined to tear Pakistan apart.

As crisis approached, Yahya, in a nationwide broadcast on November 28, 1969, promised the country a new constitution and elections. These were set for October 5, 1970, but were held in December, after being postponed by Yahya. On December 7, 1970, and January 17, 1971, the first truly representative elections in Pakistan's history took place. In East Pakistan the Awami League, which led the independence movement, won 167 of the 169 East Pakistani seats in the new National Assembly, giving them a majority of the Assembly seats. In West Pakistan, Zulfikar Ali Bhutto and the Pakistan People's Party ran using the slogan Islam our Faith, Democracy our Policy, and Socialism our Economy. They won a majority of West Pakistani seats.

The peaceful transfer of power from the military to the newly elected National Assembly depended upon Yahya and the leaders of the two parties coming to terms. Holding a majority of the seats in the National Assembly, Sheik Mujib ur-Rahman (Mujib), the leader of the Awami League, wished to assert his right to form the new government. This was unacceptable to Zulfikar Ali Bhutto. When talks between Mujib, Yahya, and Zulfikar Ali Bhutto broke down, the Pakistan People's Party decided to boycott the National Assembly. On March 25, 1971, the crisis came to a head: Mujib declared independence for East Pakistan, and the country of Bangladesh was born.

The inability of Zulfikar Ali Bhutto, Yahya, and Mujib to reach a compromise can be seen as the direct catalyst to the civil war that followed. It could be argued that as the minority party in the new National Assembly, the Pakistan People's Party should have been the one to make concessions. It could be further argued that Zulfikar Ali Bhutto, by calling for the boycott of the National Assembly, should share the blame for the civil war.

The civil war between East and West Pakistan was devastating for both sides, Zulfikar Ali Bhutto, however, benefited. On December 20, 1971, he became president and chief martial law administrator of the reduced state of Pakistan. Although the problems of East versus West Pakistan were technically solved, Zulfikar Ali Bhutto still faced many of the same problems that the country had faced in 1947.

The most pressing problem was coming to terms with India and Bangladesh. Zulfikar Ali Bhutto traveled to Simla to meet with the Prime Minister of India, Indira Gandhi, on June 28, 1972. The Simla Agreement that came out of the meeting provided for the return of Pakistani prisoners and territory captured by India during the civil war. On the negative side Zulfikar Ali Bhutto had to concede to the dominance of India's position in Southwest Asia. He also agreed that Pakistan would not seek assistance from other countries in their problems with India and Bangladesh.

With the immediate problems of India and Bangladesh solved, Zulfikar Ali Bhutto then turned to restoring the country to constitutional rule. A new constitution was drawn up and put into effect on Pakistan Independence Day, August 14, 1973. The new constitution called for a parliamentary system with stipulations that made it almost impossible for the prime minister to be removed by the legislative branch. Despite the democratic reforms, Zulfikar Ali Bhutto ruled much as his predecessors had done. Although Zulfikar Ali Bhutto had the support of the military, his main source of power stemmed from his personal charisma and the popularity of the Pakistan People's Party.

Bhutto accomplished much in his five-and-a-half years as the leader of Pakistan. He worked to break the economic hold of the so-called "Twenty-two Families." He purged the military of over 1400 officers who he feared would support yet another military takeover of the country. He reformed the civil service and the functioning of the government bureaucracy.

Two events were to cause the downfall of Zulfikar Ali Bhutto. One was his appointment of General Zia ul-Haq as army chief of staff, and the other was the elections in March 1977. In response to the call for elections, nine opposition parties joined forces as the Pakistan National Alliance. The elections were hotly contested, and the Pakistan National Alliance seemed to be riding a wave of public support. However, when the election results were announced on March 7, 1977, the Pakistan People's Party had apparently won 154 seats, and the Pakistan National Alliance had won only 38. The Pakistan National Alliance challenged the election results and called for a new election. As Zulfikar Ali Bhutto had done before, the Pakistan National Alliance now refused to join the new government. After months of turmoil, the specter of the military once again raised its head.

On July 5, 1977, the military, led by Chief of Staff General Zia ul-Haq, intervened. The military arrested many political leaders, and Zia declared martial law. Zulfikar Ali Bhutto would spend the next two years in prison wasting away at the hands of his military captors. He was eventually tried and sentenced to death on charges that were never really proven. He was hanged in prison on April 4, 1979.

4

A Child Without Equal

Eight-year-old Benazir Bhutto was trying to sleep in the upstairs bedroom of the Bhutto home at 70 Clifton Road in Karachi, Pakistan. The high, whitewashed wall, secured by barbed wire above it, circled the family house and gardens, making the young girl feel safe while her parents were away. A loyal group of servants was there to protect her and her siblings, too, both during the day and at night.

As the final evening chant from the nearby mosque (an Islamic place of worship) faded, Benazir reached under her pillow for the money her mother had given her to take care of the household. At bedtime, Benazir had secretly counted the paper rupees (Pakistan's currency) and folded her fingers over them. With her hand beneath the pillow, she clutched the money tightly and drifted off to sleep.

"Look after the other children. You are the oldest," had been her mother's parting words to Benazir as her parents left on another government trip.

During her parents' absences, Benazir took charge of her brothers, Mir and Shah, and her sister, Sanam. She was also in charge of the family home in the busy city of Karachi. This was a serious responsibility. Yet it seemed a natural duty to Benazir. It would help to shape her future character.

At both Harvard University and Oxford University, Benazir took on leadership roles. Perhaps these early experiences prepared her for an unexpected life in jail. They may also have prepared her for the responsibilities she assumed in December 1988. At the age of 35, Benazir Bhutto became the prime minister of Pakistan, and the first woman to lead a Muslim country.

Pakistan is a small country in Asia. Home to more than 110 million people today, it is wedged between Afghanistan and Iran on its western border, and India and China on the east. In the north, it is capped by the craggy mountains and sparkling lakes of India's Jammu-Kashmir Province.

Pakistan had been a part of India until August 14, 1947. At that time, India gained its independence from Great Britain. Throughout history, the different religious groups of India—the Hindus and Muslims—had fought bitterly. To try to ease this fighting, East and West Pakistan were created at the same time India became an independent country. The majority of Indian Muslims moved to East and West Pakistan, while almost all Hindus remained in India.

Ali Bhutto, Benazir's father, had been a representative of the young nation of Pakistan since the division. He was often sent out of the country. He served at the United Nations in New York City for seven years. At other times he served Pakistan as its commerce minister, foreign minister, and energy minister. All of these positions required time away from home. Benazir remembers seeing her father more in newspaper photos than in person.

Despite the long absences, Ali Bhutto cared deeply for his children, and he had a great influence on them. The birth of his first child, Mohatarma Benazir, on June 21, 1953, was a very special date in his life. Traditionally, the Muslim world has considered girls less desirable than boys, but not AH Bhutto. He adored his first-born daughter. He nicknamed her "Pinkie," because, as a baby, her skin was quite rosy and fair. Her given name, though, was to be

"Benazir," meaning "without equal" or "without comparison."

Before Benazir's birth, Ali Bhutto had been studying law at Oxford University's Christ Church College in England. His wife, Nusrat, was there with him. Ali Bhutto wanted his child to be born in Pakistan, however, so Nusrat returned to Karachi. He joined her there several months later.

Nusrat Bhutto was Ali Bhutto's second wife. In many Pakistani families, land was kept within the same family for generations by encouraging cousins to wed through an arranged marriage. Ali Bhutto had taken part in this tradition.

At the age of twelve, the young Bhutto was promised a cricket set (a British game similar to baseball) if he would marry a younger cousin. This would keep the Bhutto lands safe within the family. After the ceremonial marriage, Ali did not see his bride again, because he went away to school. Once he had finished high school, his parents sent him to study at the University of California at Berkeley. From there, he continued has studies at Oxford University in England. As an adult, Ali Bhutto saw his first wife only at family gatherings.

A Muslim man is allowed to have four wives, as long as he treats and supports all of them fairly. In 1951, Ali Bhutto married Nusrat. This was apparently a happy marriage, as Ali Bhutto never married again. Their marriage was based on equality, and Ali ignored the traditions of eating and sleeping separately from his family.

In many ways, Ali Bhutto was unlike most Muslim men. His early marriage, as well as the time spent studying in the West, made him realize how unfair many Muslim laws were to women. This may have been the reason he was attracted to an untraditional woman such as Nusrat.

Nusrat Bhutto refused to wear the burqa when she appeared in public. A burqa is a large, tent-like veil, which covers a Muslim woman's face and body. According to Islam, women are expected to cover themselves whenever they leave their homes, or when strange men are in the room. Unlike most Pakistani women at the time, Nusrat Bhutto, who was born in the neighboring country of Iran, was college-educated. Before her marriage, she had defied custom by driving her own sports car around the seaport city of Karachi.

Benazir and her brothers and sisters were born into this liberated, well-educated family. Ali Bhutto expected each of his four children to strive for higher education, too. The education of his daughters was as important to him as that of his sons. "I ask only one thing of you, that you do well in your studies," Bhutto told his children.

Despite Nusrat's own feelings against the veil, she did not want to impose her feelings on her daughters. Once, when Benazir was twelve years old, she and her mother were traveling north by train from Karachi to Larkana, the site of the family homestead. As they neared the station, Nusrat unpacked a black burqa and told Benazir she must put it on. "You are no longer a child," she said.

The view of the world from behind the veil was a shock to Benazir. The black veil made all the beautiful colors look gray. The desert heat from behind the curtain was almost unbearable.

"Pinkie wore her burqa for the first time today," Nusrat told Ali later. He was silent for quite a while before he said, "She doesn't need to wear it. The Prophet himself said that the best veil is behind the eyes. Let her be judged by her character and her mind, not by her clothing."

"My father was the dominant role in my life because he was the head of the family," recalls Benazir. "My mother was more like a peer—someone to confide in. We played card games together...I respected her."

Much of Benazir's early life was carefully planned for her by father. At the age of three, Benazir went to Lady Jennings' nursery school. When she was five years old she was sent to the Convent of Jesus and Mary, which was down the street from her house in Karachi. Like many upper-class Pakistanis, the Bhuttos felt this private school would offer a better education than a public Muslim school. In the lower grades, Benazir dressed in a simple white dress. In high school, she wore a shalwar kamiz, a uniform made up of a white tunic and trousers, draped with a green dupatta, or long scarf, from her shoulder across to her waist.

Benazir was given a very good education, and it was in school that she learned much of her English. The languages spoken within the Bhutto home were Sindhi—the language of the province in which they lived; Persian—Nusrat's native language; English; and Urdu—the national language of Pakistan.

Benazir's Urdu teacher at the convent was Humera Nairn, who recalled, "Benazir's Urdu was not so good. Her speeches today are well written, and she uses the right words, but she makes some grammatical mistakes in Urdu. I remember when she was fourteen or fifteen that she was very respectful, helpful, polite, and very sweet."

Students at the convent studied between the hours of 7:45 A.M. and 1:15 P.M., with a break for tea or a cold drink and cookies at 10:30. During the break, Benazir might play volleyball outside on the concrete playground. If her father were away, either elsewhere in Pakistan or abroad, he would telephone Benazir to check on her special school reports. In addition to their school-work, Ali Bhutto arranged for tutors to give his children lessons in math and English after school hours.

Despite these full days of serious studying, Benazir always had time to enjoy herself. She liked to play pranks on her teachers, which they recall with much amusement at the convent.

"I remember buying stink bombs in a joke shop in London," Bhutto told the girls at her old school in Karachi in 1987. "The next time we had an exam, I just passed a few of them to my friends. As soon as the exam began, we put them under our chairs and crushed them. There was such a horrible smell that our exams were delayed!"

"I think school has the most dominant influence on a person," Benazir says. "It taught us discipline, perseverance, and how to work under pressure, but there were fun times, too—times of laughter. I remember playing netball and volleyball. I even won a cup for table tennis."

When Ali Bhutto worked for the government, he lived in Rawalpindi in northern Pakistan, near Islamabad, the capital. During this time, Benazir and Sanam were sent to a branch of their Catholic boarding school in nearby Murree. Located in the mountains, Murree had been a British military post at one time, but now belongs to the Pakistan military.

To the two young Bhutto sisters, the cold winds of Murree were very different from the steamy heat of Karachi. Because the school did not have any indoor heating to combat the cold of winter, the school year ran from March through December.

In the Murree School, Benazir slept in a pink dormitory with twenty other girls. Each bed had a doll resting on the pillow. In the morning, Benazir would slip into her white shalwar kamiz with its red dupatta, brush her bangs and straight hair, and rush down the carpeted metal staircase to breakfast." After eating, she would run down the hillside steps to her classrooms, which overlooked the playing fields for soccer, field hockey, and volleyball.

In 1965, while attending the boarding school, Benazir and Sanam were witness to a war. In 1947, when India was partitioned to form India and Pakistan, the northern area of Jammu-Kashmir was given to India. Since most of the people in the area were Muslims, they felt closer to Pakistan than they did to India. This led to a seventeen-day war between the two countries. The town of Murree, overlooking the valley of Kashmir, was caught in the middle of this conflict. During the many air raids, Benazir and her friends imagined themselves kidnapped and hidden somewhere in the hills.

Benazir's father, then Pakistan's foreign minister, flew to the United Nations to plead for a cease fire. He succeeded. When Pakistan's President Ayub Khan gave Kashmir back to India at a settlement conference, though, Ali Bhutto resigned. He did not think that the president should have agreed with India's plans to keep the province.

In 1967, Ali Bhutto formed his own party, the Pakistan People's Party (PPP). He used his home in Karachi as its headquarters. Angered by this move, Pakistan's president sent Bhutto to jail in the city of Lahore.

Meanwhile, Benazir returned to the Convent of Jesus and Mary in Karachi to finish high school. She remembers herself at the age of fourteen as "very shy—I could hardly lift my eyes off the carpet and say 'hello' to strangers."

Soon, Benazir had to prepare to take her college entrance exams. She wanted to apply to the University of California at Berkeley, where her father had gone as a freshman. Instead, he insisted she go to Radcliffe, a college at Harvard University in Cambridge, Massachusetts.

"The weather in California is too nice," he told her. "The snow and ice in Massachusetts will force you to study."

After applying to Radcliffe, Benazir began to study seriously for her December 1968 exams. She felt lonely in Karachi while her mother and sister were in Lahore visiting her father in jail. But a letter from Ali Bhutto lifted her spirits.

"I am praying for your success in your... examinations," he wrote from prison. "I am really proud to have a daughter who is so bright that she is doing 0-levels [entrance exams] at the young age of fifteen, three years before I did them. At this rate, you might become president."

While in solitary confinement in prison, Benazir's father also wrote to tell her she needed to read more. "I know you read a great deal, but you should read a little more of literature and history. Read about Napoleon Bonaparte, the most complete man of modern history. Read about the

American Revolution and about Abraham Lincoln ....Read about India from ancient times. And above all, read the history of Islam." She accepted his advice.

After Benazir took her exams that December, she entered the Karachi Grammar School near her home for a term. The time passed slowly as she waited impatiently for the results of her exams to come in the spring.

5

Education

The authorities at Radcliffe College in Cambridge, Massachusetts, were concerned about Benazir Bhutto's age and upbringing. Barely sixteen, she would be coming from the protection of a strict Catholic school. Also, as a member of an upper-class-Muslim home, she had been very sheltered. The officials felt that the liberal American society might be too shocking for such a young girl from a Pakistani home. In addition, the country was involved in the Vietnam War at the time. Overall, the college officials did not think it was a good time for Benazir Bhutto to come to America.

Ali Bhutto, however, knew his daughter was level-headed and intelligent. He called upon John Kenneth Galbraith, a one-time ambassador to India, and an economics professor at Harvard. He asked Galbraith to persuade Radcliffe to allow his daughter into the university.

In the spring of 1969, a letter came from Radcliffe College. Benazir opened it, unsure about the results of her exams, but eager to know the college's decision. Happily, she was accepted.

Leaving her family and friends was hard for Benazir. As she and her mother, who would travel with her, stepped through the carved front door of their home, they uttered a prayer from the Koran, the Islamic holy book. The servants crowded around the car, sad to say good-bye to the tall, slim teenager they had protected for sixteen years. When the car left the courtyard and drove past the solid iron gates, Benazir took a final look at her home, trying to memorize its every feature.

As they drove to the airport, Benazir knew she would miss the noisy bustle of Karachi with its 2 million (more than 7 million today) people. Sadly, she realized that she would no longer hear the calls to prayer that echoed through Karachi five times a day. Benazir was frightened because she was leaving the life she knew behind, but excited at the same time.

Mother and daughter arrived at Boston's Logan Airport in the sizzling heat of an August day. They were soon crossing the Charles River into Cambridge, to find the Eliot Hall dormitory where Benazir would live.

Nusrat Bhutto spent several weeks helping Benazir settle into her new surroundings. She made sure her daughter had a complete wardrobe, full of Pakistani saris (colorful, loose-fitting dresses) and shalwar kamiz that were tailored in wool for the cold winters.

Before Nusrat left, she and Benazir went to tea at the Galbraith home near the Harvard campus. The Galbraiths would become like second parents to Benazir. She was often invited to their Cambridge home as well as their vacation home in Vermont. Because of his fatherly concern, Professor Galbraith was always available to help and advise Benazir. "John Kenneth Galbraith hovered over Benazir like a father," remembered one of Benazir's friends in later years.

Over tea that day, Benazir met Peter Galbraith, who later became a dear friend. Peter remembers their first meeting. "When she arrived at Harvard, she was a very quiet and shy sixteen-year-old. I had been hitchhiking around South America and proceeded to expound [relate] to them my theories of life at Harvard.... After I got through, I expected Mrs. Bhutto would take her daughter back to

Pakistan. Of course, I said all this with great authority, but I was barely a freshman and knew absolutely nothing. However, Pinkie did tell me years later that she was shocked at my long, stringy hair."

In fact, coming from a country where the dress code is rather formal, Benazir had a difficult time getting used to the untidy appearance of many young Americans. She found their patched blue jeans, rumpled shirts, and untended beards very strange.

After her mother left, Benazir, using her nickname Pinkie, soon found the college department store, known as the Harvard Coop. There, she bought the "uniform" of the other college students—blue jeans and sweatshirts. Although they were not the traditional clothes of Pakistan, they would let Benazir follow the Muslim custom of completely covering the body. The new outfits also kept her from being too different from her classmates.

Benazir had intended to major in psychology at Radcliffe, but she quickly changed her mind when she found out she would have to perform experiments with animals. This, she could not and would not do. She loved birds and animals, especially her two cats. Therefore, she turned to the president of Radcliffe, Mary Bunting, for some guidance. Benazir decided to major in comparative government—the study of different forms of government. This was good news to her father. He had secretly written to the president, asking her to steer his daughter in the direction of political studies.

Like most teenagers away from home for the first time, Benazir was homesick. Although the autumn leaves of New England were a beautiful sight, she missed the colors of Pakistan, as well as her family. Fortunately, the girls near her room befriended her and tried to ease the pain of homesickness.

Anne Fadiman was a friend of Benazir's at Radcliffe. She explained some of the adjustments Benazir had to make in coming from an upper-class Pakistani family. "She had always been chauffeured by a driver; her meals were cooked and served; doing her own laundry was out of the question; and answering a telephone herself was something new."

Once Benazir learned to do these things and became used to Western ways, she became more outgoing and began to blend into the Harvard University community. Before long, she was elected secretary of Eliot Hall, and was responsible for giving tours to students interested in coming to the university.

Peter Galbraith later recalled, "She was very much a joiner—on the Harvard Crimson newspaper. She gave tours. She took part in demonstrations against the Vietnam War. Her first experience with tear gas was not in Pakistan, but on the Boston Common." On the Common with her friends, Benazir stood shouting slogans and holding antiwar signs along with the other protestors.

Not only did Benazir protest against the war, she was attracted to the new women's liberation movement in the United States. At coffee shops and in the dormitory rooms, the Radcliffe girls talked about their new freedom to pursue any career they wanted. If a young woman decided not to marry, this was now considered an acceptable choice. For a Pakistani woman, these views were unusual, as well as brave. Yet, despite Benazir's independence, she would wear traditional Pakistani dress when invited to a function by Pakistani hosts.

With all these exciting outside interests, Benazir never neglected her studies. Keeping her grades high was a part of her promise to her father. She had also been influenced by the hard work required in her Pakistani schools.

"Everything was easy for her. She took care of her academic life without agonizing over it. She was always relaxed and never worried," commented one of Benazir's roommates, Yolanda Henderson.

Meanwhile, in the middle of Benazir's third year at Radcliffe, Pakistan held its first free elections in thirteen years. The voters in West and East Pakistan elected her father and the Pakistan People's Party by a great majority.

In the Pakistani parliamentary system, the prime minister is the head of the government, just as the president is in the United States. The prime minister is the leader of the National Assembly's majority party.

Pakistan also has a president. The president is the head of State and does not have the power of the prime minister. He or she acts more as an adviser. The president can be from either the Senate or the National Assembly. He or she must be elected by the four provincial assemblies, the Senate, and the National Assembly.

When Ali Bhutto became prime minister, Benazir Bhutto became an instant celebrity. When she had first arrived at Radcliffe, no one had known where Pakistan was. A year later, everyone was congratulating her on her father's victory.

Ali Bhutto's success did not last long. Sheik Mujib of East Pakistan demanded independence from West Pakistan. Geographically, the two areas were separated by almost 1,000 miles of India. There was also some disagreement about a new constitution. Sheik Mujib and many of the East Pakistanis felt Pakistani laws were unfair to them. This eventually led to a rebellion.

Benazir's feelings of pride were quickly forgotten when other students began criticizing her country. For almost two years, she defended Pakistan. At the end of 1971, Benazir was shocked when she learned the Indian army had invaded East Pakistan. They had also bombed Karachi and other parts of West Pakistan. The Indian government claimed to be helping East Pakistan gain its independence.

That December, Ali Bhutto flew to the United Nations to challenge India's military attack against Pakistan. He cabled Benazir to ask her to come to New York for sessions with the Security Council. This organization tries to settle disputes between nations. Benazir left for New York immediately. Before the Security Council met, Bhutto tested his daughter's thoughts on what the outcome might be.

"All nations will condemn India and make them withdraw their troops from East Pakistan," she said.

With a smile, Ali Bhutto replied, "You may be a good student of international law, Pinkie, but you don't know anything about power politics. One of the fundamental [basic] lessons of diplomacy is to create doubt: Never lay all your cards on the table."

Although the elder Bhutto fought hard in the United Nations Security Council, no decision was made. Losing patience, Ali Bhutto stormed out of the council chamber and returned to Pakistan. Bhutto went back to Harvard. Eventually, East Pakistan became the independent country of Bangladesh.

Because of these events, Benazir Bhutto was gaining much experience. Even her professors noticed a growing maturity and courage. "At eighteen," she remembers, "I was brash and thought I was the cat's whiskers, and I was opinionated."

A senior tutor of Bhutto's, Kevin Starr, witnessed an example of her new boldness. He saw a debate in class between Benazir and a Harvard professor over the rights and wrongs of an independent Bangladesh. Although the students and professor were against her, they admired her courage and the way she stood up for her beliefs. Her reputation soon spread across the campus.

In the beginning of her senior year, Benazir's brother Mir entered Harvard as a freshman. Remembering her own homesickness, Benazir helped Mir meet people and professors. She showed him where everything was at Harvard. When they were together, brother and sister discussed Pakistani politics and read the daily news about their homeland.

During her last year at Harvard, Benazir wrote her senior honors thesis on pink paper, and passed it out to her professors and friends. Although her years in Cambridge had been happy ones, the final days were sad. She had to say good-bye to her friends, some of whom were leaving for graduate school or to start careers.

On graduation day, Benazir's mother and Mir were there

to see her graduate cum laude (with honors) only days before her twentieth birthday. Although her father could not attend, it was a proud moment for both parents.

Hoping to stay and go to the Fletcher School of Law and Diplomacy at Tufts University, Benazir pleaded with her father. It was useless. He wanted her to go to Oxford University, where she had already been accepted.

Benazir was happy to be returning to Pakistan for the summer, but sad to be leaving America. She was comforted, though, by the knowledge that Peter Galbraith and his wife would also be attending Oxford University in the fall.

OXFORD

Benazir learned the art of diplomacy—skill in handling disputes peacefully—at her father's side. It was as much a part of her education as her lectures and tests.

One important experience occurred during the summer of her junior year at Harvard. Ali Bhutto invited her to attend a summit. "I want you to witness firsthand a turning point in Pakistan's history," he had told her. This turning point would be a meeting between Prime Minister Indira Gandhi of India and Prime Minister Ali Bhutto. The purpose of the June 1972 meeting was to solve the problems caused by India's military attack of East Pakistan. The two leaders also wanted to end the argument over which country should own Kashmir.

Meeting Prime Minister Gandhi at the parties and receptions was exciting. At dinner, Indira Gandhi stared at Benazir across the table. Perhaps she was remembering the times when she went with her own father, Jawarharlal Nehru, former Indian prime minister, to many different countries.

While Gandhi and Bhutto spent many days negotiating, Benazir wandered around the mountain town of Simla. A group of reporters usually followed her. They commented on the combination of her Pakistani and Harvard wardrobe.

It caused quite a stir and was seen as a symbol of the new generation.

Unfortunately, the talks came to a sudden halt. Neither Gandhi nor Bhutto would change their positions. Ali Bhutto told his daughter and advisers to pack and return to Pakistan.

Before leaving, though, Bhutto made one last attempt to make Gandhi change her mind. As a final gesture, the Indian prime minister agreed to give back the territory her nation had taken during the 1971 war, and later the prisoners. In this way, both governments kept their pride.

After the Simla summit, Benazir joined her father on a state visit to the United States in 1973. Ali Bhutto was to be honored at a White House dinner. In the West Room, Bhutto was seated next to Henry Kissinger, secretary of state.

Since Kissinger had been a professor at Harvard before becoming involved in the government, Benazir opened the conversation by talking about some of the problems at the university.

After dinner, Kissinger approached Ali Bhutto and told him, "Mr. Prime Minister, your daughter is even more intimidating [frightening] than you are." Ali Bhutto laughed, proud of his daughter.

This was the kind of training Benazir Bhutto brought with her to Oxford University in the fall of 1973. Ali Bhutto had great respect for Oxford University, and remembered his own years there very well. He wrote this letter to his daughter as she began her university life there. "I felt a strange sensation in imagining you walking on the footprints I left behind at Oxford over twenty-two years ago...Your being at Oxford is a dream come true. We pray and hope that this dream... will grow into a magnificent career in the service of your people."

While Benazir knew her father was happy she was at Oxford, the first months there were hard for her. Her single room at Lady Margaret Hall was small. Unlike her room at

Harvard, she had to share a bathroom with the other girls on the floor. Benazir also missed having a private telephone and much more reserved than the outgoing, friendly.

However, the pressures of schoolwork kept her busy. She had to write two essays each week for her triple majors of philosophy, politics, and economics. This did not give her time to think about her personal problems. Peter Galbraith and his wife were at Oxford for her first two years, so Benazir was not completely alone.

Benazir's father urged her to join the Oxford Union Debating Society. The debating club is one or the best at the university, dating back to 1823. Benazir was interested in joining the foreign service of Pakistan after graduation, so the debating club seemed a good place to practice her speaking skills. She liked the thrill and challenge of debating. Little did she know, then, that her future life would require all the debating skills she learned at Oxford.

In her formal Pakistani dress, she delivered her first speech at the Oxford Union on the need to impeach, or remove from office, President Richard Nixon. Although Benazir had previously supported President Nixon in his foreign policy, the Water-gate investigation changed her attitude. She presented her case so well that the students voted to impeach Nixon 345 to 2. Her debut was a great success.

Benazir's association with the debating club helped her form strong friendships with people such as Victorial Schofield, who would later write a book about Ali Bhutto. With all these interesting activities to keep her busy, Benazir soon became fond of the narrow, winding cobblestone streets of Oxford.

Oxford University was begun in the twelfth century, when a group of scholars and monks decided to form a college of higher learning. The university is made up of a series of small, self-governing colleges. The colleges are based on the tutorial system. Under this system, each student must write one or two essays a week on each subject, and then discuss them with an individual tutor. These assignments kept Benazir busy. She also attended lectures, did research, and was active in the debating club.

Despite this heavy workload, Benazir did have some free time. She had a yellow sports car her father had given her as a graduation present from Harvard. She could be seen driving the small British MGB convertible around the streets of Oxford. Often, the windshield was covered with parking tickets and personal notes from friends. According to one of her tutors, "That yellow car was her signature around Oxford. 'There's Benazir Bhutto,' everyone would say."

On weekends or holidays, she would drive up to London, only an hour away. Here, she would treat herself to her favorite peppermint stick ice cream. At times, she might drive to Stratford-on-Avon to see a Shakespearean play. Besides these day trips, there were parties and picnics, boating on the river, or garden parties at the boathouse.

"She worked hard, played hard, and made lots of friends," recalls Elizabeth Chilver, principal at Lady Margaret Hall.

Because of her intelligence and enthusiasm, Benazir's Oxford tutors thought she might become an ambassador's assistant at the United Nations. Yet they did not consider her anything but a normal student. Her tutor in politics, Gillian Peele, remembers Benazir as "a bubbly sort of character, charming, and a stylish dresser... She was hardworking, but it cannot be said she was a perfect... undergraduate."

Absorbed in the British college life, Benazir seemed happy. Yet her private thoughts were a little different. "When I became twenty-one," the prime minister said wistfully, "I was sad to leave my teenage years in becoming an adult."

As an adult, Benazir found herself having to deal with adult problems. Before she had left for America, her father had warned her, "You might find prejudice in the West."

Benazir's first encounter with racial prejudice came not in America, but at the London airport.

She had made a quick trip to Pakistan to attend an Islamic summit planned by her father. While waiting in line to go through immigration and customs upon her return to England, the immigration official made some racial remarks. "How can a Paki have enough money for an Oxford education?" were his parting comments.

Angry and shocked, Benazir refused to reply to his question. She snatched her papers away from him and walked quickly and proudly from the airport. This was her first experience with prejudice, and she began to realize that people saw her country and its residents differently than she did. This attitude both saddened and disappointed her.

Like her time at Harvard, the three years at Oxford passed quickly. This time, though, Benazir was eager to leave school and get started in "real life." But her father insisted she return to Oxford for another year to study international law and diplomacy. Ali Bhutto felt his children must be twice as good as others, because they had had many advantages in life.

Benazir returned to Oxford in 1976. This time, she studied at Saint Catherine's, which had been built in 1962. To Benazir, it did not have the same feeling of history as her old school, Lady Margaret Hall. It did have an interesting mix of foreign students, though. Also, Saint Catherine's offered a degree in international law and diplomacy, which Lady Margaret Hall did not.

Benazir's brother Mir would be a first-year student at Oxford now, so once again, she had a family member close by. She was also looking forward to her last year at Oxford because she could now campaign for president of the Oxford Union Debating Society. No woman or non-British person had ever been given this honor before.

Changing attitudes toward women had taken a long

time to reach the debating society. Ten years before, the ratio of men to women had been seven to one. Despite these odds, Benazir ran for president. She was elected the club's president and began serving the three-month term in January 1977.

After her victory, a cable came from her father. "Overjoyed at your election as president of the Oxford Union," he wrote. "You have done splendidly. Our heartwarming congratulations on your great success."

Before taking on her duties as club president, Benazir and Mir flew home to Pakistan for the winter vacation. The trip began well, with a celebration for Ali Bhutto's birthday at the family home, Al-Murtaza. This one-story house and sprawling gardens were hidden behind high, cream-colored walls and a bright green steel gate near the town of Larkana. In the town, camels and water buffalo lumbered through the winding streets.

At the birthday party Banazir was introduced to Zia ul-Haq, who was being considered as her father's chief of staff. After first meeting Zia, Benazir felt uncomfortable. She did not like the way he flattered her. Silently, she wondered why her father had chosen him.

During the party, father and daughter went for a private walk. They strolled under the archways of the sculptured hedges, through the rose gardens, and past the swimming pool and small zoo with its deer and birds. They discussed politics, as they often did. Ali Bhutto told Benazir of his plans to hold elections in March instead of August. He hoped this would help him begin working on the many projects in which he was interested.

One of these projects included equal rights for women in the foreign and civil service. In fact, he had already appointed a few women to important posts. Ali Bhutto also wanted to pass a land reform act, allowing Pakistan's farmers to grow more crops and receive higher pay for them. Overall, he was determined to improve the quality of life for the growing number of poor people in Pakistan.

Benazir agreed with her father's plans, and soon flew back to Oxford.

As president of the debating society, Benazir successfully organized and ran four serious debates. When the fifth and final debate arrived, tradition called for it to be light and amusing. A rock and roll musical was the choice. The title was "This House Likes Dominating Women," set to the tune of the song, "Jesus Christ, Superstar," and nicknamed "Bhutto's Bye Bye Song." At the end, Benazir was lifted onto the shoulders of her fellow students and carried out of the hall.

Meanwhile, the political campaign in Pakistan had become violent and emotional. From Oxford, Benazir and Mir listened to radio reports and read the Pakistani newspapers mailed to them. The night of the March election, they waited for a telephone call from their father. To their relief, they soon learned Ali Bhutto had won.

But the post-election riots by the Pakistan National Alliance (PNA) threatened the country and Ali Bhutto. Britain's Scotland Yard came to Oxford at one point and warned Benazir her life might be in danger, too.

"There was little we could do, in an open site, to protect her," recalls Principal Chilver. "She was given her own telephone, so that she could report anything suspicious, but her best protection was provided by her fellow students, who kept...watch. She herself was not alarmed and took the threats calmly."

Despite these problems, Benazir still felt carefree enough to celebrate her twenty-fourth birthday by giving a party at Oxford. Ruby red strawberries and frothy whipped cream were offered to her many friends. After this party, Benazir said her good-byes and returned to Pakistan to join her family in Rawalpindi. There, she hoped to begin her diplomatic career by finding a job in one of the government offices.

6

Death of Her Father

During the summer of 1977, each of the four Bhutto children returned to Pakistan from various points in the world. They met at their father's official residence, a white mansion set in beautiful grounds in Rawalpindi, near Islamabad.

Islamabad has been the capital of Pakistan since 1959. Once a sleepy mountain village, modern Islamabad has a population of more than 250,000 people. The city has wide boulevards lined with modern office buildings and shops. The four, pencil-thin spires of the Faisal Mosque rise above the skyline. From almost every location in the city, there is a sweeping view of the chalk-white parliamentary buildings. The wood-paneled Senate has a portrait of Mohammed Ali Jinnah—the founder of Pakistan—as its focal point, hung above the speaker of the House. The 80 members of the Senate are elected every six years by the four provinces—each province having an equal number. Its powers are limited. In contrast, the National Assembly, similar to the House of Representatives, has the power to pass laws and approve the budget. There are 237 Assembly members, each of whom serve five-year terms. The number of Assembly members from each province varies according to that province's population.

When Benazir stepped off the airplane in Islamabad

and into the arms of her father, he said, "Thank God you've completed your education and are home. Now you can help me." After spending eight years in school, those were the words Benazir wanted to hear. She was now ready to work for her country.

Within a matter of days, Benazir moved into a small office near her father's at the secretariat and began sorting through his files. Considering her education, she was starting in a lowly position. Yet she felt useful and ready to learn as much as she could about the government and her father's political responsibilities.

What seemed like an ideal beginning to her career was about to be destroyed. On the night of July 7, 1977, the Rawalpindi household was suddenly shaken out of a quiet sleep.

"Wake up! Get dressed! Hurry!" Benazir remembers her mother warning. "The army's taken over!"

In a state of fear, Benazir ran to her parents to find out what was happening. Nusrat said that a coup d'etat, or overthrow of the government, by General Zia had taken place.

While Nusrat explained their situation to the rest of the family, Ali Bhutto contacted General Zia. Zia said that he intended to hold another election in ninety days, and that Ali Bhutto was under house arrest. An official car was on its way to the house to take Ali Bhutto to his place of detention.

Shocked by the news, Ali Bhutto thought of his family. He instructed Nusrat and the children to return to the family home in Karachi. Benazir's mother suggested the two boys, Shah and Mir, leave immediately, and perhaps even leave Pakistan. They might be in danger as the sons of the arrested prime minister.

The Bhuttos waited for Zia to come and take the prime minister away. During the long delay, they packed their things. The tense atmosphere was broken by a sharp cry from Nusrat Bhutto. When Benazir and her siblings ran downstairs, they saw Ali Bhutto looking out of the window of a black Mercedes. He was trying to say good-bye. He was soon out of range as the car disappeared through the gates.

The comfortable, safe life of Benazir Bhutto was suddenly in danger. As she stood and watched the car disappear from sight, she recalled the last conversation she had had with her father that evening. He had asked if she believed General Zia would actually hold elections in ninety days as he promised.

"Yes, he will," she had said without hesitation. Her father had called her naive, and explained in harsh words that a government seized by the army did not promise much future for democracy. Zia had ignored the constitution of 1973, and Ali Bhutto to thought he would not give up power easily

General Zia had promised Bhutto he could stay anywhere he desired. This was not the case, however. Bhutto wanted to go to his home in Larkana. Instead, Zia sent him to the colonial rest house in the jagged hills of Murree, where the Bhutto family had spent many vacations. Zia believed that this faraway location would keep Bhutto out of politics. Despite these moves by the new government, both Ali Bhutto and the PPP remained popular.

With General Zia in control of the country, a kind of religious extremism was practiced. During the month of Ramadan, Muslims are not allowed, according to their religion, to eat or drink in public between sunrise and sunset. Normally, if a Muslim breaks this rule, he or she is seen as unfaithful. Zia, though, threatened to arrest and punish anyone who broke their fast.

As expected, the Bhutto family was under a great strain at this time. But for Benazir, at least, this experience prepared her for situations she had not encountered before. One lesson she learned was how to deal with journalists. They called the Karachi home constantly for information about her father. Ali Bhutto simply said, "Invite them all to tea."

Following his advice, Benazir asked an eager group of reporters into the crowded dining room, attempting to correct the many rumors that were spreading around Karachi and elsewhere. There was even one rumor that said Ali Bhutto was responsible for the summer rains that were drowning and damaging the farm crops. Another rumor accused Benazir Bhutto of carrying a video camera in her handbag to film illegal political meetings.

During the press conference, Benazir tried to answer as many questions as she could. Later, when talking with her father, she told him of the silly rumors she had heard. He advised her to go immediately to the city of Lahore, where most of the people had suffered ruined crops. This would be a good political move to show that the Bhuttos cared.

Benazir was frightened by his suggestion at first. Yet when she and her brother finally went to Lahore, they were surprised at the overwhelming reception they were given. At one point, Ali Bhutto himself telephoned a public meeting in the city to express his sympathy to all those who had lost crops in the flood.

Because of Ali Bhutto's continued popularity while still in captivity, General Zia decided to release him. The Bhutto family was reunited in Karachi. As happy as Benazir was at their father's freedom, she openly expressed her feelings against Zia. Her father spoke sharply to her about this.

He believed everything they said in their house was being recorded. "You are careless," he told his daughter. "You are not in a democracy of the West now.

The excitement at Bhutto's release was soon overshadowed by Zia's attempts to jail Bhutto again on a false accusation. Benazir was caught in the middle of one of these plots before dawn on a September night in 1977. Five men in white suddenly forced open her bedroom door at the Karachi home and pointed machine guns at her. Not only did they threaten her, but they smashed everything in her room.

Meanwhile, Ali Bhutto was escorted out of the house to military headquarters. Benazir dressed quickly and went with him, despite their attempts to leave her behind. She spoke bravely in her father's defense, but, once again, Ali Bhutto was placed in jail. The judge, however, could not find enough evidence to find him guilty, and Ali Bhutto was set free.

Ali Bhutto was eager to return to campaigning. He warned Benazir again about speaking against Zia when she said, "You're going to win the elections and try General Zia for treason." Since he had told her before about the electronic "bugs," this outburst angered him.

Unfortunately, Ali Bhutto's problems were not over. He was again seized by the army and taken from his house in Larkana. He was put in Sukkur Jail briefly before being moved to Karachi Central Jail, and then to Lahore.

While Ali Bhutto was being moved from jail to jail, Nusrat Bhutto campaigned as a candidate to replace her husband. Such a step is traditional for political families in Asia. Benazir, too, found herself thrust on stage to give speeches. Although frightened by the crowds, she used everything she had learned at Oxford and tried to hide her fear.

Threatened by the popular response to the Bhutto women, Zia placed Benazir under house arrest for fifteen days. Nusrat Bhutto continued to speak out in public, now saying, "My daughter is used to wearing jewelry. Now she will be proud to wear the chains of imprisonment."

During the time she was under house arrest, Benazir burned most of the Bhutto family photos. She did not want the army to find them and use them in any way.

When she was released, Benazir and Nusrat rented a house in Lahore to be near Ali Bhutto during his trial. Benazir became frustrated and angry by the things she heard. The only response and comfort were the words from her father. "You can imprison a man, but not an idea."

Further arrests and detentions (being held by the police) awaited Benazir and Nusrat during the trial. At one point, Zia ordered the massacre of any people who supported Bhutto. While facing these hardships, both England and America seemed very far away to young Benazir. All she could do was worry behind the walls of her Karachi home.

At the moment her father was found guilty of murder and sentenced to death, Benazir used her wits to find ways to see him in the Rawalpindi District Jail, and her mother in Lahore. She managed to smuggle messages from Ali Bhutto out of his jail. The messages usually contained advice on how to protest legally against her detention. This advice was rewarded when Benazir was released. Soon after this, though, she had an operation to cure a painful ear infection.

While she was recovering, Benazir's twenty-fifth birthday arrived. To celebrate, she and her mother went to Ali Bhutto's jail. There, Benazir found her father in good spirits, though much thinner than the last time she had seen him. Despite the annoying insects and crawling lizards in the cell, her father teased her and said, "You are twenty-five now and eligible for office." They looked at each other and laughed.

Benazir had decided it was up to her to prepare a legal case to defend her father against the death sentence. To cope with the piles of legal documents, she asked her Oxford friend, Victoria Schofield, to come to Pakistan to help her.

In February 1979, Ali Bhutto delivered a plea in court to remove his death sentence. The plea was denied. Bhutto was sent back to jail despite messages from Great Britain, the United States, and Saudi Arabia on his behalf.

On April 3, 1979, Benazir and her mother were taken to see Ali Bhutto for the last time in the compound of the Rawalpindi Jail. Through the iron bars, the three of them had only thirty minutes to say their good-byes. His last words to Benazir were, "You don't know how much I love you, how much I've always loved you. You are my jewel. You always have been."

The government reported that on April 4, Ali Bhutto was hanged. Benazir, however, believes he may have been killed in some other way because there were no hanging marks on his neck. The real truth may never be known.

As a part of Muslim tradition, Nusrat Bhutto began four months of private mourning. The military would not bother Nusrat, but what of Benazir? She did not know what would happen to her. Whatever it was, she decided she would never give up her father's ideals or his political cause.

Under heavy guard, Benazir and Nusrat Bhutto were taken to the family burial ground in Larkana to pay their final respects to Ali Bhutto. The grave was only a mound of mud without any identification. Through their tears, the women scattered flower petals over the freshly shoveled mud.

Benazir felt stronger after this emotional event. Everything her father had taught her took on new meaning. "Stand up to the challenge. Fight against overwhelming odds. Overrun the enemy. What you make of your destinies is up to you." These were just a few of his words of advice.

Not long after their visit to the grave and their return to jail, mother and daughter were allowed to go to their home in Karachi. Both women were relieved to be home, where they could once again smell the welcome sea breezes.

With the public mourners for Ali Bhutto crowding into the gardens at 70 Clifton, Benazir began to think about how she could carry out her father's mission. She turned the house into the business headquarters for the PPP. Here, Benazir personally conducted meetings for the party from early in the morning until deep into the night. Party members respected the Bhutto name, so they felt satisfied with Benazir leading the party.

The PPP's efforts to win local elections throughout the country were successful, but the national election against Zia was their main focus. They decided to oppose Zia even without Ali Bhutto. This constant threat of opposition forced Zia to cancel the scheduled elections.

Angry at the continued support for the PPP, Zia moved the Bhutto women to Larkana in 1980 and put them under strict house arrest for six months. This was the seventh time Benazir had been arrested in two years. Although this imprisonment was at Al-Murtaza, they were not allowed to have visitors or to talk on the telephone. Also, any mention of the Bhuttos in newspapers was forbidden by the government. The Bhutto family was still a powerful force in Pakistan. Zia hoped that if their names were not mentioned, people would forget about them.

Within the walls of Al-Murtaza, boredom was Benazir's biggest enemy. Nusrat and Benazir's only contact with the outside world was a shortwave radio that received broadcasts from the British Broadcasting Corporation (BBC). In December 1979, when they heard that Pakistan's neighbor, Afghanistan, had been invaded by the Soviet army, Benazir was stunned. This news deepened her worry about her two brothers. When they had fled Pakistan at the time of the coup, they moved to Afghanistan.

Added to these worries and the increasing boredom, Benazir and Nusrat were facing the first anniversary of Alt Bhutto's death. Their request to visit his grave was denied.

Benazir needed something to keep her busy. She decided to turn all her energies to challenging her six-month detention in court. Her study of law at Oxford, and her father's legal advice in the past, gave her the necessary courage. Benazir and Nusrat were soon free and on their way back to Karachi. Without wasting any time, Benazir became involved in the PPP again. This time, though, Zia's intelligence force followed her and watched her every move.

Benazir continued to have annoying problems with her ear, which interfered with her political work. She worried about the possibility of deafness. To help Benazir recover, Nusrat suggested her daughter go back to Larkana and take over the running of the family farm. It had been seriously neglected since the coup d'etat almost two years before.

For a woman in Pakistan, this assignment was remarkable. But Benazir had little choice: her father was dead, and her brothers were both hiding in Afghanistan. No Bhutto male could do it. So, Benazir traveled to Larkana and took on a landowner's responsibility. She covered every inch of the flat stretches of land with a jeep and supervised the acres of rice paddies and sugarcane fields.

Benazir's physical and mental problems lessened with these new chores. The people who worked for her had not been managed by a Bhutto family member for two years. Under her direction, the farm prospered.

Pakistani farmland is a rich resource. The 800-mile Indus River nourishes the flat wetlands, where rice and vegetables are grown. On the drier side of the river, cotton and sugar are raised. Benazir was learning firsthand about the problems faced by the farmers.

At the end of a long day in the fields, Benazir refused to relax. Her evenings were filled with visitors who brought news from the political world, and students who came to speak with her. Many dealt with her as an equal, and she felt she was one of them. Because of her position as a landowner, villagers, too, came to her to settle their personal and marital problems. She disliked making decisions for a married couple, and this was the least favorite part of her job.

Meanwhile, the government was becoming even more strict. Freedom of the press was limited, and political activists were arrested. Nusrat decided the only way to beat Zia in 1980 was for the PPP to unite with a certain section of the opposing party, the PNA. When the two groups came together for discussions, the meeting lasted seven hours. The outcome was called the Movement to Restore Democracy, or the MRD.

Having become very cautious since her father's murder, Benazir distrusted this new organization. But people throughout Pakistan supported the MRD.

The MRD, as well as the continued opposition to his rule, threatened Zia's government. Police broke up a secret meeting of the MRD in the northern part of Punjab Province. There, Nusrat was arrested and sent back to Karachi.

Benazir and her mother had made an agreement that the two of them would never appear at the same meeting together. After their last detention, Nusrat had said, "There is no use in both of us landing in jail again at the same time, so you keep a low political profile. That way, one of us... can stay on the outside to lead the party."

The military rulers were becoming increasingly frustrated with the MRD and the Bhuttos for encouraging the strikes across the country. On March 7, 1981, police searched for Benazir in Karachi all night and the next day. They even invaded the homes of some of Benazir's closest friends. Some were just questioned, and others were put under house arrest.

On this particular night, Benazir was spending the night at a friend's house while Nusrat held a political meeting at 70 Clifton. In the middle of it, the police forced their way in and arrested Nusrat, demanding to know where Benazir was staying. She would not tell them.

As they searched throughout Karachi, the police located Benazir the next day at the home of Nusrat Bhutto's doctor. Benazir was later to learn that Zia had not only arrested her, but six thousand MRD supporters as well.

Not knowing what would happen to her, Benazir was sent to Karachi Central Jail. Five hours later, she learned that her own mother had been placed in a cell without any running water or bedding.

Benazir was kept five days in this jail. On March 13, 1981, in an attempt to frighten her, the police drove her through Karachi to the airport with the sounds of screaming sirens. She was put on an airplane without any explanation as to why and where she was going. On board, she was given a newspaper to read. One of the articles reported that a Pakistani airplane had been hijacked in Afghanistan, and the hijackers were demanding the release of fifty-five Pakistani political prisoners. One military man and one passenger were shot before the plane was forced to fly to Syria. The article suggested her brother Mir had planned the hijacking. Terrified, Benazir finally understood why she and her mother were being treated as they were. General Zia and the military thought the Bhutto women were involved in planning the hijacking.

Benazir was flown out of Karachi to Sukkur Jail, far away in the Thar Desert. Here, her cell seemed more like a cage, with barred doors on two sides and barred windows on four sides. At night, there was no electricity, and she shivered as the cold winds swept across the desert and whipped through the open bars of her cell. Without blankets or warm clothing, the cold bothered her, making it hard to sleep on the rope cot.

Being separated from people and other prisoners made her feel ill and depressed. She decided she must find things to do to keep herself occupied. Everything Benazir did, from brushing her hair to brushing her teeth, had a set routine. This way, each moment of the day had a purpose.

Benazir did not like the prison food. She was given watery soup and tea with some bread. Sometimes, the guards offered her pumpkin or fish. Finally, unable even to try to eat the food, she stopped eating altogether.

To avoid the long hours with nothing to do, Benazir began keeping a daily diary in a small notebook. It had been secretly given to her by a sympathetic jail keeper. Carefully, she recorded events inside and outside the prison. Fortunately, some of her jailers could be trusted. They took the notes away every day and hid them safely. Benazir was also allowed to read one newspaper every day, which she read over and over again.

Each day, her captors warned her of a possible trial and death sentence. During the five months she spent in Sukkur Jail, Benazir continued to grow thinner. Worried that she might die in jail, the police shifted her back to the Karachi Central Jail, where she hoped to see her mother. Instead, she was pushed into a dark, dirty cell. To her surprise, she was taken to a hospital the next day. The guards said she had uterine cancer. She had known nothing about this, and had not given her consent for an operation.

At the hospital, Sanam was permitted to visit her for thirty minutes. She found Benazir drugged, screaming about her father's death, and fears of her own death.

Two days after her operation, Benazir was flown back to Sukkur Jail. Years later, Benazir heard that a former Pakistani minister in the PPP received a telephone call in London about the government's attempt to kill Benazir Bhutto on the operating table. The minister immediately gave a press conference and reported this information to the London newspapers. Benazir does not know for certain if her death was Zia's intent, but she feels sure the public attention helped to save her life.

Meanwhile, the Pakistani newspapers were making terrible accusations against Mir and Shah for heading a secret organization called Al-Zulfikar from Afghanistan. The articles also claimed that Nusrat and Benazir knew about this. Benazir was angered, especially when she heard that Zia was arresting and torturing those who had any connection to the name of Bhutto.

Within her jail cell, Benazir was suffering from a different kind of torture. The daytime heat in May soared to 120° F (48° C). The hot desert dust swirled into her cell, crusting her face. Her skin cracked and peeled, and unsightly blisters appeared on her face. Without the proper diet, her hair began to fall out in clumps, too.

At this point, Benazir says her jail officials began suggesting suicide as a way to end her physical suffering.

They told her that her party leaders and followers were deserting her. "I prayed to God to give me strength," she said later. To her jailers, she said, "If I am the only person left resisting the tyranny of the regime, then so be it. I don't believe your lies."

In this weakened condition, Benazir celebrated her twenty-eighth birthday. Her sister Sanam was the only visitor. Sanam brought some happy news at last—she planned to marry Nasser Hussein, a longtime friend of their brothers. Benazir could not have been happier for her sister, feeling that this step would help protect her. Nasser had a successful telecommunications business, and Benazir thought he was a good person.

After Sanam had left, Benazir turned to prayer. Each day she hoped for a miracle. Then one day, the matron of the jail opened the gate to her cell and told Benazir she was leaving.

For a moment, Benazir was hopeful. Perhaps she would at last be allowed to return to her home in Karachi. There, she would see her mother, who had been sent home recently after having been found coughing up blood in her Karachi cell.

The police vehicles screeched out of Sukkur Jail, sped over the canal locks, and raced along the crumbling tarmac to Sukkur airport, where Benazir was placed on a plane to Karachi. There, she was met by army vehicles that passed the turn-off to her home, dashing her hopes for a family reunion.

7

Home Again

The year 1985 ended on a positive note in Pakistan for those in opposition to General Zia: On December 30, General Zia lifted martial law. Many saw this as another positive step toward a return to democracy. Feeling pressure from the West, General Zia had nine months earlier set up an advisory national assembly. Although political parties were still outlawed, many of the seats in the assembly were won by people loyal to the Pakistan People's Party, and nine of Zia's cabinet members failed to get elected. Many in the opposition refused to participate in Zia's plans as long as he continued to control the military and hold it as a threat over anyone who went too far in questioning the government.

The first real test of Zia's new liberalization came when antigovernment demonstrations broke out throughout the country. The demonstrations on January 5, 1986, marked the fifty-eighth anniversary of the birth of Zulfikar Ali Bhutto. General Zia, still the army chief of staff, kept the troops home and permitted the demonstrators to denounce him and his government. Despite the appearance of the changes, many in the opposition pointed out that General Zia was still firmly in control and could easily reinstate martial law at any time. Benazir Bhutto characterized the changes as cunning camouflage intended to convince the West, especially the United States, that democracy and human rights were returning to Pakistan.

The only way that Benazir Bhutto and her followers in London could test the resolve of the Zia government's move away from martial law and toward democracy was to return to Pakistan and make their demands for total democracy. General Zia had set 1990 as the date for the next national elections. Benazir Bhutto and the Pakistan People's Party, along with the other groups that made up the Movement to Restore Democracy, hoped to force General Zia to schedule elections sooner and to give them the opportunity to defeat him in open and free elections. Shortly after the lifting of martial law, Benazir Bhutto and a number of her followers in London decided they would return to Pakistan. Some of those working with her in London had cases pending against them in Pakistan, and their return would really test Zia's resolve. Benazir Bhutto knew it was a mistake to give General Zia a chance to prepare for her arrival, so the actual date for the trip was kept secret.

Prior to returning to Pakistan, Benazir Bhutto made three trips. She visited Washington, Moscow, and made a religious pilgrimage to Mecca in Saudi Arabia. Benazir Bhutto claims that her trip to Washington was to draw attention to the upcoming test of democracy in Pakistan. Many believe that she also went to Washington to assure those in power that if she were successful in her plan to democratically overthrow General Zia, she would support United States interests in the area. Without at least the tacit approval of Washington, it is doubtful that Benazir Bhutto would have been able to stand up to General Zia.

Her trip to Moscow, at the invitation of a women's organization, was seen as an indication of Benazir Bhutto's political savvy. The visit to Moscow placated many of the left-leaning members of her party who viewed the United States as part of the problem because of their long-term support for General Zia. In addition, it probably strengthened her position with the United States, who would want to keep Benazir Bhutto out of the Soviet sphere of influence.

It was at this time that Benazir Bhutto caught the eye of the media. Her impending and hopefully triumphant return to Pakistan made great news. Benazir Bhutto took advantage of the media attention to challenge Zia's guarantees of liberties. She appeared on many television news shows in Europe and the United States and was interviewed by the BBC on the radio. The BBC put her on the air in both English and in Urdu, the official language of Pakistan, for broadcast over the BBC affiliates in Pakistan.

As the preparations for Benazir Bhutto's return proceeded, she began to hear that if she returned to Pakistan, she would be assassinated. Rumors came in from all parts of Pakistan, and one of the Bhutto family servants at 70 Clifton desperately tried to contact Benazir Bhutto in London. When she finally got the message that he had something urgent to tell her and tried to call, she was dismayed to learn that the man and his young niece had been brutally murdered. Considering the number of people that General Zia had had killed because of their opposition to his rule, Benazir Bhutto was wise to take the threats seriously. She couldn't be stopped, though, and on April 11, 1986, she once again returned to Pakistan.

This time there was no veil of mourning. Finally, Benazir Bhutto and the Pakistan People's Party had a position of strength to speak from. They couldn't lose. If General Zia permitted them to speak openly, they would be able to rally the people around their cause and force open and free elections. If General Zia reinstated martial law and tried to smother the opposition, he would prove that his reforms were a farce. Many thought that a return to martial law would send the masses into the street and bring about a violent overthrow of the Zia government. The test was coming, and as Benazir Bhutto and her party members made final arrangements to land in Lahore, the capital of the Punjab and the home of General Zia and many of those in the government and the military, people began to flock to the city.

By the time the Pakistan International Airlines plane landed in Lahore, there were millions of people in the streets of the city. Lahore had taken on the atmosphere of a carnival. After almost nine years of repressive military rule, the people of Pakistan had something to rejoice about. Benazir Bhutto represented the hope for the future. The massive outpouring of emotion and support amazed all: the press, the government, the opposition parties, and Benazir Bhutto were all impressed by the largest gathering in the history of Pakistan. It took the motorcade, carrying Benazir Bhutto on a platform in the back of an open truck, ten hours to travel eight and a half miles from the airport to the site chosen for Benazir Bhutto to speak.

The crowds showered Benazir Bhutto with flower petals and gifts as she traveled to the Minar-i-Pakistan; a monument to Pakistan's independence that had been built while her father was prime minister. In her speech she called for new elections which would be open and free from the type of restrictions that General Zia had placed on the elections that had selected the current national assembly. She went on to compare General Zia with the recently deposed leader of the Philippines, Ferdinand Marcos. She predicted that Zia would become another Marcos, bowing to the will of the people and leaving the country. Benazir Bhutto had frequently compared herself to Corazon Aquino, who had defeated Marcos after she had taken over her assassinated husband's party. Although the comparison made good copy for the media, it was rather superficial. There were many more differences than similarities between the situation as it had existed in the Philippines and the situation in Pakistan.

Later that week, while Benazir Bhutto was meeting with the leadership of the Pakistan People's Party and other opposition political leaders, armed gunmen broke into the house where Benazir Bhutto was supposed to be. Fortunately, she was elsewhere at the time, but as one member of her party said in describing the gunmen, "They weren't looking for a cup of tea." To capitalize on her overwhelming reception in Lahore, Benazir Bhutto decided to make a tour from Lahore to Peshawar. She wanted to take her message to as many people as possible before the holy month of Ramadan began. During this period of Ramadan, all Muslims are supposed to fast during the day and limit their activities.

During the first few weeks that she was back in Pakistan, Benazir Bhutto began to show a side of herself that surprised many and worried those she opposed. She showed the world that she was able to electrify the huge crowds that greeted her wherever she went, while at the same time she walked a very thin line that held together most of the factions of her party. At the age of thirty-two, Benazir Bhutto was proving herself to be a superior politician. In her speeches she continually called for elections to be scheduled before the planned date of 1990 and presented a balanced and sensible plan for the future of Pakistan. After nine years of being a prisoner and an exile, she amazed the world with her abilities, and many believed that she would be able to ride this wave of support to the leadership of her country.

The old guard of the Pakistan People's Party, many of whom had been supporters of Zulfikar Ali Bhutto, at first, saw Benazir Bhutto as a figurehead they could use to rally the masses to the party and against General Zia. However, Benazir Bhutto's success and popularity with the people was so great that she became the actual leader of the party. To solidify her leadership of the party she found it necessary to oust some of the old guard politicians and to replace them with younger members who were loyal to her. This led to some fighting in the party and charges that Benazir Bhutto would turn out to be the same sort of autocratic leader that her father had been and that General Zia was. With her wide appeal among the people, Benazir Bhutto was able to weather the storm within her Party and to solidify its position.

The month of Ramadan lulled the government into a false sense of security, and General Zia's handpicked prime minister, Mohammed Khan Junejo, went so far as to say that Benazir Bhutto and her party had fizzled. It is true that things were quiet during Ramadan, but that was for religious reasons, not because Benazir Bhutto had lost the support of the people. As Ramadan ended, the Pakistan People's Party and the other group involved in the Movement to Restore Democracy renewed their call for elections. They pressed for national elections to be held before the end of 1986.

As Benazir Bhutto and her party began to renew their activities after Ramadan, it became apparent that the fragile, unspoken truce between the Zia government and the opposition was beginning to deteriorate. July 5, 1986, marked the ninth anniversary of General Zia's coup and was declared Black Day by the opposition leaders. Demonstrations were organized all over Pakistan, and in a number of places demonstrators clashed with the police. In Sind, three people were killed and hundreds were wounded when the police fired on the crowds. Elsewhere, others were injured by club-wielding riot police.

The opposition leaders used this as an illustration of the true nature of the Zia regime and proof that General Zia would allow the opposition to protest only under his terms. When both sides planned mass demonstrations for Pakistan Independence Day, August 14, 1986, it appeared that the opposition forces and General Zia were headed for a confrontation.

Benazir Bhutto was reluctant to take her movement into the streets where the peaceful protests she had led would become violent. However, she was maneuvered into leading the Independence Day demonstrations in Karachi by the other leaders of the Movement to Restore Democracy. They put her in the position where if she did not participate it would look like she was bowing to government pressure. At first. Prime Minister Junejo said he would keep his own Pakistan Muslim League members home on Independence

Day to avoid a conflict and asked the opposition to do the same. As August 14 approached and it became obvious that the opposition parties were going ahead with their plans, Junejo ordered the demonstrations canceled and placed a three-day ban on public demonstrations. General Zia, in what many viewed as a feeble attempt to make it look as though he wasn't involved in the decisions to limit the rights of the demonstrators, was on a pilgrimage to Mecca at the time. Most believe, however, that Prime Minister Junejo was in frequent contact with General Zia, who was actually running the show from Saudi Arabia.

On August 13, 1986, the inevitable police crackdown on the opposition began. Over one thousand party leaders were arrested and held without being charged with crimes. Out of fear or confusion, Benazir Bhutto was missed in the roundup on August 13, 1986. Some believe that the government did not want to confront Benazir Bhutto and the large contingent of Pakistan People's Party members who surrounded her home at 70 Clifton, which is in an area where there are many foreign embassies and where many foreign diplomats live.

As August 14 dawned, close to five thousand party members had gathered at 70 Clifton in an attempt to protect their leader. Benazir Bhutto awoke on this morning to her followers chanting "Long live Bhutto" and "Our sister Benazir." With the press in a vehicle in front and Benazir in a second vehicle following, the crowd surged into the streets and headed for the market area of Karachi where Benazir Bhutto was scheduled to speak. They had not gone far before the police began their onslaught. The police launched tear gas at the vehicles and unsuccessfully tried to disperse Benazir Bhutto's entourage. In Benazir Bhutto's vehicle they were able to close the windows and sunroof before the gas got to them. Benazir Bhutto was given a wet towel to cover her eyes. However, the sunroof of the vehicle carrying the members of the press jammed, and they received a serious dose of tear gas. Some of the reporters didn't fully recover for a number of months.

By switching vehicles and sending out doubles to elude the police, Benazir Bhutto was able to carry out her Independence Day plans and to speak to the thousands of people who had gathered near the markets to hear her. The police continued their rampage, launching, by some counts, as many as three thousand canisters of tear gas in Karachi alone, where at least four people were killed by police gunfire. There were other incidents of violence throughout the country.

After a day of playing cat and mouse with the police, Benazir Bhutto was arrested late in the afternoon of August 14 during a press conference at 70 Clifton. She was handed a thirty-day detention order and taken off to solitary confinement at Landhi Borstal Jail, which is a juvenile detention center on the outskirts of Karachi. Apparently there was no room for her at Karachi Central Jail, which was overflowing with political prisoners. It was later learned that the orders for her arrest had come by telex directly from General Zia in Saudi Arabia.

Benazir Bhutto's arrest on that day was seen by many as a vindication of her stand that General Zia, along with the police and military, were still running the country and could at any moment return to the repression that had characterized most of Zia's reign. Many in the press saw the harassment and arrest of Benazir Bhutto as a major victory for the opposition. Although the United States government had always been one of Zia's staunchest supporters, in carefully worded statements. United States spokesmen expressed disappointment in the apparent backward step that the Zia government was taking in its process of democratization. They specifically expressed dismay at the arrest and imprisonment of Benazir Bhutto.

In the aftermath of the August 14, 1986, Independence Day demonstrations, the conflict between General Zia and those who opposed him intensified. In the first five days following the arrest and imprisonment of Benazir Bhutto, official sources admitted to twenty-two people having been killed in demonstrations while the opposition claimed as many as forty had been killed by government forces and over ten thousand people arrested. In one incident, train service north of Karachi was disrupted when militants loyal to the opposition sabotaged the train lines.

By August 20, 1986, General Zia once again turned the military against the people of Pakistan. Troops were deployed along the sabotaged rail lines and elsewhere in Sind province. Four top Pakistan People's Party members were charged with murder in the deaths of four people in Lahore. The story had a familiar ring to it. The opposition claimed that the four dead had been part of an antigovernment demonstration and were shot down by police. The police claimed that the opposition leaders shot four pro-government demonstrators.

As the violent demonstrations continued, one thing became clear: Benazir Bhutto's support was strongest in her home province of Sind. The lack of support from the Punjab wing of the party was reopening old wounds caused by earlier ethnic violence and the favoritism that General Zia had shown to his home province of Punjab. It would be Benazir Bhutto's job to heal the wounds within the opposition.

As August 1986 came to an end, General Zia was again firmly in control of Pakistan. Benazir Bhutto and most of her fellow opposition leaders were in jail. Those not in jail were unable or unwilling to risk further deaths, tear gassings, and beatings at the hands of the police and the military. At a press conference in Islamabad, Pakistan, on August 30, 1986, General Zia made it clear that he and his supporters in the military had a very limited amount of tolerance for those who wished to speed up the democratization process. He went on to say, without offering any proof, that he had substantiated evidence that Benazir Bhutto was being backed by the Soviet Union. This seemed to many a futile attempt to discredit Benazir Bhutto.

By early September the street violence that had rocked

Pakistan for the last two weeks of August had died out. Benazir Bhutto was scheduled to appear in court on September 10 to face charges. On September 9 she was released from jail and allowed to freely return to her home at 70 Clifton. Some claim that General Zia did not want to give her the forum of an open courtroom in which to speak out against him. Many other opposition leaders were released at the same time.

In her first meetings with party members after her release from jail, Benazir Bhutto advocated restraint and hoped that she could lead a movement to bring about change peacefully. Had she done otherwise she could easily have plunged Pakistan into a pattern of escalating violence on both sides. In many ways it would have been easier to unleash the masses. It took strong leadership and foresight for Benazir Bhutto to choose the path she did.

The fall was spent solidifying the Pakistan People's Party's internal organization. Benazir Bhutto spent the time touring the country and gathering support for herself and the Pakistan People's Party. In October 1986, Benazir Bhutto announced that she was temporarily canceling her call for immediate elections. Some of the old guard of the Pakistan People's Party split off and formed the National People's Party headed by the former Sind Party leader and general during the reign of Zulfikar Ali Bhutto, Ghulam Mustafa Jatoi.

Ironically, the greatest challenge to the Zia government came not from the political opposition but from ethnically motivated disturbances throughout the country. During the fall, troops had been called upon to deal with ethnic violence in the Northwest Frontier Province, Baluchistan, Lahore, Punjab, and finally in Karachi. The rioting in Karachi apparently began with the attempt by the government to crack down on drug dealers among the Pathan minority. The crackdown set off violence between the Pakhtuns and the Muhajir, people who had moved from India to Pakistan when Pakistan became a country. Before the military was able to establish an uneasy peace in the area, more than

170 people had been killed and 2,000 arrested. The months of ethnic violence culminated in the resignation of all thirty-three members of the federal cabinet and placed the process of returning Pakistan to civilian rule in a doubtful light.

Despite the violence among the various ethnic factions in the country, Benazir Bhutto had much to celebrate as the New Year, 1987, dawned. This would be the first New Year's Eve in six years that she was both free and in Pakistan. Support for her party was growing, and the regime was proving itself unable to run the country without the strong hand of the military. There was, however, one dark cloud on the horizon of the New Year. Reports of plans to assassinate Benazir Bhutto became more and more frequent and came from sources inside and outside the government.

During the month of January, the rumors of attacks on Benazir Bhutto and those close to her turned to reality. One of her security guards had his car forced into a dead-end street in Karachi where he was shot at. A Movement to Restore Democracy leader was murdered with an axe. Others among those close to Benazir Bhutto began receiving phone calls in the middle of the night. A direct attack came on January 30, 1987, when Benazir Bhutto's motorcade was attacked by gunmen on the road from Karachi to Larkana at three-thirty in the afternoon. Fortunately, Benazir Bhutto had sent the vehicles on ahead so that she could attend a last-minute meeting in Karachi. The Pajero, a jeeplike vehicle in which Benazir Bhutto always rode, escaped through a shower of bullets. The second vehicle carrying Benazir Bhutto's security staff was stopped, and the people in the car were kidnapped.

The assassination attempt set off another rash of demonstrations against the government. The Zia regime claimed that the attack had been perpetrated by dacoits, highway bandits, common in Pakistan. As there was no ransom demand made, very few found the government's version of the story believable. Those captured in the attack were later released and claimed that their captors said they were working for General Zia.

In many ways, Pakistan was at its lowest point in many years in the early months of 1987. General Zia's plan to return the country to democracy had all but ended. The local elections in the fall of 1986 had been the most corrupt in the history of Pakistan. The hope that General Zia would ever allow free and open elections in 1990 or at any other time seemed dim. Benazir Bhutto, the Pakistan People's Party, and the other groups involved in the Movement to Restore Democracy continued their organizing and resistance to General Zia. The most important thing to happen to Benazir Bhutto in 1987 was in her personal life.

The Marriage of Benazir Bhutto

Benazir Bhutto had always planned to marry. Having experienced the early years of the women's movement at Harvard, she saw no reason why she couldn't have a political career and be a wife and mother. But events interrupted any possibility of her finding the right husband and getting married. During the time her father was on trial and appealing for his life, there were no thoughts of husband hunting. During this time her family did receive inquiries from families with sons who were interested in Benazir Bhutto. Following the death of her father, Benazir Bhutto was in jail and would not have been able to get married had she received any serious proposals. Once she was in exile, however, the inquiries from prominent families began again.

In Pakistan, as in other Muslim countries, there is little opportunity for dating in the Western sense, and arranged marriages are an accepted way for couples to get married. Her father had had an arranged marriage when he had been in his teens and then had later married Benazir Bhutto's mother for love. Her brothers and sister had all married for love. Benazir Bhutto had always expected to follow the rest of her family and to marry for love. Benazir Bhutto's life, however, had not allowed her the luxury of finding someone whom she loved and wanted to marry. Her position as the leader of the Pakistan People's Party made it impossible for her to have any social life. Even the slightest breach of Muslim custom would have been ammunition for General Zia and the government-controlled press.

A possible solution to this dilemma appeared early in the summer of 1985 when Hakim Ali Zardari approached Benazir Bhutto's Aunt Manna, the eldest member of the Bhutto family. He suggested that a marriage be arranged between Benazir Bhutto and his son Asif Zardari. Benazir Bhutto is the same age as Asif Zardari. He had also attended school in England and was from another one of the powerful landowning families of Sind Province. His father had been a supporter of Zulfikar Ali Bhutto and was the vice-president of the Awami National Party, which is one of the parties in the Movement to Restore Democracy.

At the time of the proposal, Asif Zardari ran his family's construction company and played on his own polo team, the Zardari Four. Following the customs of the arranged marriage, Benazir Bhutto's mother and aunt investigated the possibilities of the match. They delved into the Zardari family's history and financial holdings and explored all the aspects of Asif's personality and upbringing. They had even received assurances from the prospective groom that he would not interfere with Benazir Bhutto's political ambitions. Their final conclusion was that Asif Zardari would make the best match possible for Benazir Bhutto.

They approached Benazir Bhutto with the proposal and the recommendation that she accept while they were all in Cannes on the French Riviera in July 1985. The death of her brother Shah Nawaz Bhutto at that time put any thoughts of marriage out of everybody's mind. But Benazir Bhutto's aunt and mother kept the idea of a marriage between Benazir and Asif alive. In November 1986, Benazir Bhutto's Aunt Manna included Asif Zardari on the guest list of a dinner party at 70 Clifton. Without making the connection between the man whose family was trying to arrange a marriage with her and the man that her aunt introduced her to at 70 Clifton, Benazir Bhutto proceeded to get into an argument with him.

As time passed, the Zardaris continued to press for the marriage, as did Benazir Bhutto's mother, sister, and aunts. Finally starting to give in to the pressure applied by her family, Benazir Bhutto began to make inquiries of her own about Asif Zardari. The more she learned about this persistent man, the more the possibility of their getting married became a reality for her. Finally, Benazir Bhutto agreed to meet with her suitor. Unlike most arranged marriages, in this one the prospective bride would have the final say.

The meeting was planned for July 22, 1987, at the apartment of Benazir Bhutto's Aunt Behjat in London. Over the next few days, Asif Zardari and Benazir Bhutto were together, although never alone, at a number of family social gatherings. Finally, Benazir Bhutto, the leader of the opposition to General Zia in Pakistan, educated at Harvard and Oxford, agreed to an arranged marriage with Asif Zardari. Their engagement was announced in London on July 29, 1987. They expected that the wedding would be held before the end of the year.

The road to marriage had been different for Asif Zardari. He had known for many years that he would like to marry Benazir Bhutto. During an interview in London, Asif Zardari surprised Benazir Bhutto by admitting that, when they were both in their early teens, he used to watch her when she came to a movie house that his father owned. He had admired her from afar since that time. Apparently he had told his father five years earlier that if his father wanted him to get married then they should arrange it so he could marry Benazir Bhutto.

The engagement of Asif Zardari and Benazir Bhutto had immediate ramifications for the Zardaris. The Central Bank, which was controlled by the Zia government, canceled loans to the family businesses. The Zia-controlled press printed false stories that were intended to discredit the engaged couple. Rumors were spread that Benazir Bhutto would abandon politics now that she was to be a wife. It was much more wishful thinking on the part of the Zia government than reality. In many ways, being married strengthened Benazir Bhutto's bid to lead her country. She proved to many of her critics that she was more than willing to accept the traditional customs of her country while 'still trying to bring progress.

After the announcement of their engagement, Benazir Bhutto continued to work as the leader of the Pakistan People's Party. Her goal was to have as large a base of support as possible by the time of the 1990 elections. As Benazir Bhutto traveled about the country, Asif Zardari kept in touch with her by calling frequently. Through the phone calls, they began to get to know each other. They set the date of their wedding for December 19, 1987 and chose to hold it at 70 Clifton, the Bhuttos' home in Karachi.

As the plans became finalized for the wedding, it became apparent that, despite the traditional nature of the arranged wedding, Benazir Bhutto was going to put her own stamp on the proceedings. In Pakistan, families frequently spend their life savings and then go into debt to make a wedding as elaborate as possible. As the leader of a political party that was hoping to improve the lot of people in Pakistan, Benazir Bhutto wanted her wedding to set an example of moderation. She hoped that other people would see that if Benazir Bhutto could cut back on wedding expenses, so could they.

Benazir Bhutto allowed her prospective husband to buy her only two outfits for her trousseau, as opposed to the traditional twenty-one. Rather than wearing solid gold bangles from wrist to elbow, as is the custom, Benazir Bhutto wore a few gold bangles and then covered her arms with inexpensive glass bangles that she bought in the bazaars of Karachi. It was also traditional that the bride's wedding outfit be covered with as much gold brocade as possible. Benazir Bhutto told Asif that she wanted her wedding clothes to have brocade only at the top or the bottom but not both. She also asked her prospective husband to show restraint in buying jewelry for her to wear at the wedding. She wanted just a few pieces rather than the lavish amounts that most Pakistani brides wear. She also intended to keep her last name. She felt it necessary as the leader of the party founded by Zulfikar Ali Bhutto to keep the Bhutto name.

The prewedding emotions among the political observers and activists in Pakistan were mixed and often reflected which side of the political battle lines a person was on. Those who supported General Zia and Prime Minister Junejo saw the wedding as Benazir Bhutto's abandonment of her cause. They hoped that as Mrs. Zardari, Benazir Bhutto would fade from the political scene. Most of those who supported her seemed to share in her joy as they would if their sister were getting married. This is how many in the movement saw Benazir Bhutto—a sister who had borne the brunt of the tragedies that had befallen their country since General Zia had taken over. To many it was the unofficial end to the period of mourning that had begun with the execution of Zulfikar Ali Bhutto in 1979. The emotional outpouring surrounding the wedding forces one to conclude that Benazir Bhutto had made the right choice as far as her political life was concerned. The wedding also made Benazir Bhutto more acceptable to many of the more conservative elements in Pakistan who could never have supported her as a single woman in a male-dominated society.

The plans for the wedding included two separate activities. The first was a private wedding for two thousand people to be held in a tented garden near 70 Clifton. The second was a public reception in the sports stadium in Lyari, a poverty-stricken area of Karachi that is a Pakistan People's Party stronghold and the site of Benazir Bhutto's Independence Day speech on August 14, 1986. Because of her sisterly image, most of the young men who made up the bulk of the Party felt they should be invited to their "sister's" wedding. The reception at Lyari was intended to include as many supporters as possible. For the first time since 1977, the Pakistan People's Party would have something to celebrate.

The private part of the wedding, despite Benazir Bhutto's attempts to tone it down, was a lavish affair attended by many of the wealthiest people in Pakistan. The guest list also included three of Benazir Bhutto's friends from the United States and six from her days at Oxford. As if to highlight the public nature of Benazir Bhutto's life, she held a press conference the morning of the wedding. She wanted to explain to the reporters that had flocked to Pakistan what her plans were and why she had decided to go ahead with her marriage. Benazir Bhutto stressed that she did not expect those from the West to understand her motivations for accepting an arranged marriage. She explained that her choice was not between an arranged marriage or a Western-style romantic marriage but between an arranged marriage or no marriage at all. She further explained that she had an obligation to her family and the customs of her country to marry and have a family.

On the subject of a family, she said that Asif wanted a large family, but that they would wait to have children until after the 1990 elections. She did relate to the reporters that one of her friends had told her that the best way for Benazir Bhutto to get General Zia to call for early elections was to become pregnant as soon after the wedding as possible

The wedding consisted of two days of ceremonies that are traditional to Muslim weddings. After the actual vows were said on the second day and the invited guests were greeted at the reception by the newlyweds, Benazir Bhutto and her new husband headed for Lyari. At the public reception, over one hundred thousand people had assembled to celebrate the marriage of Asif Zardari and Benazir Bhutto. One reporter stated that it was more like a rock concert than a wedding reception. The newly married couple sat on a stage that had been specially built for the occasion. They were dressed in the matching white tunics that they had been married in. The massive crowd shared the joy of the day and celebrated as fireworks burst in the sky above.

Many of the celebrants waved their rifles in the air as they danced and fired their rifles into the skies.

One person attending the reception was killed by a stray bullet, and thirty people were injured in the crush to get close to the newlyweds. If the reception at Lyari was any indication of how the rank and file was going to react to the wedding of their leader, then it was clear that the people were happy with Benazir Bhutto's choice in her arranged marriage to Asif Zardari.

1988—The Year of Victory

The first few months of 1988 saw Pakistan become increasingly unstable. Violence was becoming a way of life for much of the country as various factions clashed. More than one hundred people died in the Northwest Frontier Province area of Gilgit when Sunni and Shiite Muslim groups fought. As many as 100 people were killed in one day of fighting between native Pakhtun tribesmen and Muhajirs, descendants of the Indian Muslims who chose to settle in Pakistan when it was created in 1947. In various locations, the military had been confronted by civilians who were disgruntled with the military's role in police activities

In some parts of the country, drug dealers and smugglers with automatic weapons were in control. The expanding drug trade during the almost eleven years of General Zia's reign had increased the number of heroin addicts from a few thousand in 1977 to nearly a million in 1988. Through all of this, recently married Benazir Bhutto continued to organize and strengthen her Pakistan People's Party. The party had suffered a serious blow in the November 1987 local elections, when they only had a strong showing in rural Sind districts. It was Benazir Bhutto's intention to get the Pakistan People's Party in a position to beat Prime Minister Junejo and President (General) Zia in the next scheduled elections in 1990.

Many people in and out of Pakistan doubted that General Zia would ever permit open and free elections. They felt this was especially true if it meant that Benazir Bhutto would end up in a position where she would have a say in the running of the country. During this time, Benazir Bhutto and her followers challenged General Zia in every way they could. The general tried to force all political parties to register and to be approved by his government. Benazir Bhutto took her case to the Pakistani Supreme Court and challenged his right to do that under the current constitution. In a ruling in February 1988, which set the court in opposition to the man who had appointed them, the Pakistani Supreme Court ruled in favor of Benazir Bhutto and the Pakistan People's Party.

General Zia was slowly losing control of the country that he had single-handedly run for almost eleven years. His hand picked prime minister and national assembly that existed at his discretion were pushing for a greater role in governing the country. On May 29, 1988, in what appeared to many to be a last-ditch effort to hang on to his power, General Zia brought the country back under his sole domination. Prime Minister Junejo returned from an overseas trip to be greeted by the announcement that General Zia was relieving him of his duties. He also dismissed the entire cabinet and dissolved the National Assembly. General Zia cited the inability of the Junejo government to handle the increasing violence in the country as the reason for their dismissal. He also claimed that there was widespread corruption in the government. The violence was self-evident, and the corruption was highly probable. In published reports, it had been repeatedly claimed that about two-thirds of the aid for the Afghan rebels were being siphoned off in Pakistan before it reached those it was intended to help. It seemed that the main reason for the shake-up was that General Zia and his military backers were unable to share control of the country with civilian authority.

There was another catalyst for the dissolution of the government and the promise of elections as outlined in the constitution. Four days earlier, a Karachi paper had leaked the news that Benazir Bhutto was pregnant and that the baby was due in the fall. If the elections came at about the same time the baby was due, Benazir Bhutto's ability to campaign would be greatly diminished. Without her visibly at the head of the campaign, the Pakistan People's Party's effect on national elections would be greatly diminished. The world will never know for sure if General Zia was motivated to act by the announcement that Benazir Bhutto was pregnant, but it seems a strange coincidence.

In mid-June, in another move that might be interpreted as an attempt to block the campaign of Benazir Bhutto,

General Zia declared a change in the basic laws of Pakistan. He put Pakistani law under the auspices of the religious leaders. Had this move been successful, General *Zia* would have turned Pakistan into another religious state like the Islamic Republic of Iran. Under the Shariah, Islamic law, the role of women in Pakistan would have been greatly diminished. The Shariah states that women are not permitted to work outside the home and must be fully covered when they leave their homes. General Zia had been pushing the country toward becoming a fundamentalist Islamic state during his entire reign. Yet this was such a drastic move and so poorly planned that even few of his supporters among the religious conservatives were able to support his call for Shariah. Loudest among the opposition to General Zia's call for Shariah were the various women's organizations in Pakistan who had fought hard for their rights in a male-dominated society. It seemed that General Zia had lost much of the political expertise that had kept him in power for eleven years. Reporters found him lacking confidence and indecisive in his press conferences.

Benazir Bhutto and those in the opposition began to prepare for the elections. They called for outside observers to insure that General Zia kept his promise of open and free elections. Benazir Bhutto's pregnancy also continued, with the due date a carefully guarded secret. Benazir Bhutto carried her medical records with her so that the secret police would not be able to get them from her doctor's office.

The truth was that the baby was due in mid-October, but Zia's intelligence forces estimated that the due date was November 17. General Zia scheduled elections for November 16, 1988.

By the beginning of August 1988, it looked as though the Pakistan People's Party candidates would be winners in any fairly held election. Many candidates who had been in the National Assembly that General Zia dissolved, switched from former Prime Minister Junejo's Muslim League to the Pakistan People's Party. They did this so that their names on the ballot would be accompanied by the symbol for the Pakistan People's Party. In a country where as many as 80 percent of the population is illiterate, the symbols on the ballot are extremely important. General Zia wanted to try to prevent a sweep by the Pakistan People's Party and to be forced to share the government with Benazir Bhutto. He declared as he had done in 1985 that the fall elections would be conducted on a nonparty basis. This turned out to be another miscalculation on the part of General Zia, as it unified the opposition against him. With Benazir Bhutto in the vanguard, the opposition called on the Supreme Court to rule on General Zia's attempt once again to ban political parties.

Many in Pakistan thought the pattern of Pakistan history was repeating itself and that either General Zia or someone else in the military would return the country to martial law rather than let a liberal civilian government come to power. The conditions in the country were such that the continuation of aid from the United States was in jeopardy. Many in the government and especially the military had legally and illegally gotten rich from the billions of dollars that had been poured into Pakistan by the United States to support General Zia in his position against the expansion of communism in Southwest Asia. As the situation neared the boiling point in August 1988, one as yet unexplained event radically changed the power struggle within Pakistan. On August 17, 1988, General Zia, accompanied by the United States Ambassador to Pakistan, Arnold Raphel, U.S. Brigadier

General Herbert Wassom, the United States military attache in Pakistan, and a number of high-ranking Pakistani military officials, were killed in a plane crash. The group had attended a demonstration of the United States-made Abrams M-1 tanks in Bahawalpur, 330 miles south of Islamabad and were returning to the capital. Shortly after takeoff, at 3:46 P.M., observers on the ground claimed to have seen black smoke coming from the plane's fuselage. Then the plane literally fell out of the sky. When it hit the ground, it bounced twice and then on the third bounce burst into flames. The fire was so hot that no one could get near the plane. All thirty people on board perished in the crash.

Theories on what happened abound. General Zia had many enemies, and most believe that some sort of foul play was involved. Many theories have come out as to who was responsible for the crash and why. The Soviet Union was suspected because of their anger regarding General Zia and the United States aiding the mujahedin in Afghanistan. The Soviet-backed regime in Kabul, Afghanistan, was suspected for the same reason. Some suggested that factions within India could have benefited from the death of General Zia and the chaos it might cause in Pakistan. Many Indians believed that General Zia was arming Sikh rebels in Pakistan and helping them in their campaign against the Indian government. There were also many suspects within Pakistan. Members of the military had staged at least one unsuccessful coup attempt against General Zia in the early 1980s. This possibility was given weight by the fact that factions within the military would have found it easiest to sabotage the plane. Mir Murtaza Bhutto, Benazir Bhutto's brother, may have been responsible. Mir Murtaza Bhutto had stated that he had tried five times to have General Zia killed. Maybe his sixth attempt was successful. The list goes on to include a number of ethnic and political factions in Pakistan and even the U.S. Central Intelligence Agency. A thorough investigation has never been completed, and it is unlikely that we will ever know the whos, whys, or hows surrounding the death of General

Zia. We can, however, assess the results of his death and the impact it had on Pakistani politics.

Under the Pakistan constitution, the president of the Senate is next in line to the presidency. Ghulam Ishaq Khan was the man who was president of the Senate when General Zia had dismissed the government in May. He became the acting president until a new government could be formed following the November elections. As many of the top military commanders had been on the plane with General Zia, there was confusion in the military as well. Acting President Ishaq Khan appointed General Mirza Aslam Beg to the post of army chief of staff, the position that General Zia had been given by Zulfikar Ali Bhutto. An advisory council was set up consisting of Acting President Ishaq Khan, General Beg, and other current and former officials. This may have been the most critical time in the history of Pakistan. It amazed many observers that Pakistan stayed calm following the death of General Zia. Two hundred thousand attended General Zia's funeral on August 21, 1988, in Islamabad. Among them was Secretary of State George P. Shultz, who represented the United States.

Many observers inside and outside Pakistan expected the military to take over and to continue to run the country, as it had done a number of times in the past. Others saw this as the first real opportunity for democracy in Pakistan. The death of General Zia also created a dilemma for Benazir Bhutto.

She and the Pakistan People's Party had been fueled for the last eleven years by one primary goal: the removal of General Zia from power and the restoration of democracy. The plane crash eliminated the major issue of the party and forced the elections into a debate based much more on issues. At the same time Benazir Bhutto was forced to direct some attention to her pregnancy. Shortly after the death of General Zia, she became worried about the well-being of her unborn baby.

She felt that the baby was not moving around enough

in the womb. Apparently, the seemingly endless meetings were taking their toll. Toward the end of August, after one meeting that lasted exceptionally long, Benazir Bhutto felt ill and went to the doctor for a checkup. Rather than visit one of the doctors who catered to the wealthy people of the Clifton area of Karachi, Benazir Bhutto had selected a doctor at Lady Dufferin Hospital in the Lyari section of Karachi. The poor people of Lyari had been the stalwarts of the Pakistan People's Party. Benazir Bhutto wanted to show them that the hospital in their part of town was as good as any.

When Benazir Bhutto went to the doctor, he did an ultrasound, which showed that there was too little amniotic fluid in the womb. This condition was preventing the baby from moving as much as it should. The doctor suggested that all the time spent sitting in meetings was causing Benazir Bhutto to have poor circulation. He had Benazir Bhutto spend the next four days in bed. She was then to follow a regimen of spending one hour each morning resting and trying to feel the baby move. She was told that if she couldn't feel the baby move, then she was to go immediately to the hospital. The doctor also wanted her to come to his office every four days so they could do a fetal stress test.

On September 19, 1988, during a regular checkup, the doctor said that Benazir Bhutto had another three or four weeks to go before the baby was due. The following day, when a fetal stress test was done, the doctor admitted her to the hospital. A seven-pound baby boy was born on the morning of September 21, 1988, by cesarean section. The happy parents named their new son Bilawal, which means "one without equal." As soon as she was able after the birth of her son, Bilawal Ali Zardari, Benazir Bhutto was back on the campaign trail.

On October 2, 1988, the Supreme Court of Pakistan ruled that political parties would be allowed to participate in the upcoming elections. The caretaker government of Ishaq Khan accepted the ruling. It seemed that even the natural environment was testing the people of Pakistan as floods swept down the Indus Valley and engulfed Lahore. In one area the government dynamited a flood-control dike flooding one of the poorer sections of the city in an attempt to save a wealthy part of the city. The people of the country were outraged.

The violence that had been plaguing the country flared again in October 1988. In early November Benazir Bhutto's mother, Nusrat Bhutto, was shot at while campaigning in Multan. This and other incidents caused many of those on the campaign trail to fear that the military would step in. However, under the leadership of General Beg, the army stayed away from the political arena. They seemed to be willing to let the election process run its course. With more than thirty registered political parties, the campaign became hectic as parties and candidates switched alliances and sides, trying to improve their chances in the elections. The coalition of parties that made up the Movement to Restore Democracy had a falling-out. The Pakistan People's Party was suddenly thrust from opposition status to front-runner. Now they were the party to beat, and many of the other parties were negotiating an alliance against them. Many were speculating that Benazir Bhutto would be the next prime minister, even though she had had to leave the campaign trail to have her baby and to overcome a kidney infection that followed.

As the elections drew closer, it became clear that it was going to be primarily a two-party race between Benazir Bhutto and the Pakistan People's Party and former Prime Minister Mohammed Khan Junejo, Mian Nawaz Sherif, and a coalition of right-leaning parties called the Islamic Democratic Alliance. The Muslim League was at the head of the alliance. The positions of the two main parties were really not that different. Both called for a better life for the poor, continued support of the Afghan rebels, close ties to the United States, nuclear power for peaceful means only, and civilian rule unhindered by the military. One area they differed over was the extent to which the country should be run according to Islamic law. The Muslim League and its Islamic Democratic Alliance were for the continued

Islamization of the country. Benazir Bhutto felt that there should be a separation of church and state. She was especially fearful that women would suffer under strict adherence to Islamic law. The main issue of the election in many ways became one of loyalty to two dead former leaders of Pakistan. Those loyal to the memory of Zulfikar Ali Bhutto would vote for the Pakistan People's Party candidates led by Benazir Bhutto. Those loyal to the memory of General Zia would vote for the Muslim League and its Islamic Democratic Alliance led by former Prime Minister Junejo. Despite everything, there were many in Pakistan who had prospered under the rule of General Zia and felt that his type of autocratic rule was needed in order for the country to remain stable. As the campaign went on, many candidates who had been loyal to General Zia tried to disassociate themselves from him.

Not having held open and free elections for over eleven years, there were no facilities or expertise in the area of pre-election polling. As the elections approached, it was hard for the media to read the electorate accurately. Many people suggested that at best the Pakistan People's Party would have a clear majority in the 237-seat National Assembly. Others expected that they might not have a majority of the seats but that they would win more seats than any of the other parties. The election process was further complicated by a separate vote for the provincial assemblies where a total of 483 seats were up for grabs. The national elections would be held on Wednesday, November 16, 1988, with the provincial elections to be held on Saturday, November 19, 1988.

As the results were tallied from the voting on November 16, it became clear that Benazir Bhutto's eleven-year quest to return Pakistan to democracy was finally succeeding. The Pakistan People's Party won 92 of the 217 seats that were to be chosen in the election for the National Assembly. The Islamic Democratic Alliance, the second largest winner, only got 55. The remaining 70 seats were scattered among a vast array of parties with the recently formed Mohajir

Quami Movement coming in a surprising but distant third with thirteen seats. An additional twenty seats in the National Assembly are reserved specifically for women and were to be chosen later.

Without a clear majority for the Pakistan People's Party, it fell to Acting President Ishaq Khan to decide whom he would ask to form the new government. As Ishaq Khan delayed his decision, the Islamic Democratic Alliance and the Pakistan People's Party headed by Benazir Bhutto vied for the support of the seventy non-committed members of the National Assembly. After the women's seats were apportioned, the Pakistan People's Party controlled 105 of the 237 seats in the National Assembly and had the support of enough independent candidates to be able to command a majority. On December 1, 1988, President Ishaq Khan invited Benazir Bhutto to become prime minister and to form a new government. In his public address to the country, President Ishaq Khan said that Benazir Bhutto had "the best qualities of leadership and foresight as a statesman." He went on to say that, "Ms. Benazir Bhutto has the country's love in her heart." His announcement officially ended the rule of the deceased General Zia and his military allies. Although Zulfikar Ali Bhutto had been the first elected prime minister of Pakistan, he had originally come to power at the invitation of the military. Benazir Bhutto became the first head of Pakistan to assume power through the electoral process.

8

Enters Politics

Imprisonment

The army convoy switched on their sirens to force their way through the traffic of Karachi until they drove into the familiar compound of dried, baked earth. Ahead was the Central Jail, a sturdy looking fortress trimmed in blue. There, Benazir entered the first iron gate and climbed through a hole in the red and blue steel door into a dark hall. This led to the superintendent's office. From there, she squeezed through another hole into an open-walled compound. She was pushed through the final gate into a cell that had once held her own mother. The feeling of depression on that August day in 1981 was almost more than she could bear.

Benazir's cell was inside a locked courtyard. All the prisoners had been moved out of the adjoining cells, leaving her alone except for a jail matron. The cell was smaller than the one at Sukkur Jail. The walls were peeling, and the ceiling fan didn't work. Only the barred windows gave off limited light and air. Benazir could hardly breathe from the wet heat of the Karachi summer.

"Sometimes in jail," she recalls, "I would indulge in self-pity and say to myself, 'Why do I have to suffer so much?' Then, I would feel guilty and focus on God and be grateful. I used to cry in my pillow at night."

The dead silence at night was even more frightening than being locked in jail. After sunset, she thought she heard noises and voices, but her guards told her she was imagining the sounds. These words reminded her of her father's jail terms. People had walked on the roof of his cell, attempting to break his calm and make him think he was going mad. Once Benazir realized this, she began praying regularly, trying to ignore all of the sounds. They eventually stopped.

Longing to see her mother, Benazir was finally allowed a short visit from her. She was shocked at Nusrat Bhutto's appearance. Benazir had remembered her mother as elegant and beautiful, not as this thin, old woman with gray hair. Because of the listening guards, the two women talked mostly about Nusrat's health. According to the doctors, she was suffering from either tuberculosis—a lung disease—or lung cancer.

After Nusrat left, Benazir felt even more lonely than she had before. She began to think about her family's misfortunes: she was in solitary confinement, her father was dead, her mother was ill, and her two brothers were somewhere in a distant land.

The only way to dismiss these thoughts of self-pity was to focus on events outside her world. She did this by reading newspapers. From them, she learned that the United States was now taking notice of Pakistan because of the Soviet invasion into Afghanistan. Before this, the U.S. government had withdrawn aid from Pakistan for fear it was developing its own nuclear bomb.

When Ronald Reagan defeated Jimmy Carter in the 1980 presidential elections, the U.S. government began providing money to Pakistan again. In order to prevent the Soviet forces from pushing over the borders into Pakistan, the United States supplied General Zia with millions of dollars and supplies. Reportedly, Zia kept large amounts of this aid for himself. He told the world that Pakistan was fighting communism. A spokesperson for the American State Department called him a "world statesman" and a "benevolent [kindly] dictator." Further aid came from international food organizations to help support the Afghan refugees entering Pakistan.

As Benazir sat in her cell and read about Zia becoming a hero in the eyes of the Western world, she was torn between discouragement and anger. Unable to think about the political situation in Pakistan without becoming enraged, Benazir tried to concentrate on her sister's wedding. It would be held in Karachi on September 8, 1981. The jail superintendent offered to free her for the wedding if she would give up politics completely. Benazir refused.

On the evening of the wedding, the prison matron came to Benazir suddenly and told her she had permission to go to Sanam's wedding. In a daze, Benazir was taken in a train of police cars to 70 Clifton. As she stepped into the courtyard at the front entrance, she was greeted with the scent of jasmine and roses, and the sounds of festive music. Her relatives, who had come from as far as California, England, France, and all parts of Pakistan, rushed to embrace her.

Benazir's first step was to take a hot bath. As she tried to wash away the grime from weeks in her unsanitary cell, she began to put aside the hardships of jail. Sipping the pure, cold water was another luxury she had missed.

Benazir spent the next two days reading international and national publications, and talking with her mother and sister. Benazir was happy that Sanam's was not an arranged marriage, as was typical in Pakistan. Nasser Hussein had risked the displeasure of his family in marrying Sanam. They considered the Bhutto name a dangerous one. Nasser and Sanam had stood up for themselves, though, and Benazir was very glad for them.

As part of the traditional wedding ceremony, the reddish brown henna dye, called *mehndi,* was used to paint beautiful scrolls and pictures on the hands and feet of the ladies. Under a canopy, the wedding couple sat on cushions inlaid with tiny sparkling mirrors. The guests chanted songs about the conditions of the marriage, and what each partner would do for the other.

The police interrupted the ceremonies several times, serving notices to Nusrat and, in general, trying to upset the Bhutto family. Benazir had become so used to their methods and to her life in prison that she caught herself referring to the jail as her home.

Ignoring the police disturbances, the wedding continued. The bride and groom were each asked three times if they agreed to the marriage. At the end of the marriage vows, the couple looked into a mirror placed between them to recognize their new married state. Watching them, Benazir felt her eyes fill with tears.

When the ceremony was over, Benazir hastily wrote a letter to Peter Galbraith, her friend from Harvard and Oxford. She had learned during the wedding that he had come to Pakistan, demanding to see her in jail. He had carried with him a letter from the Senate Foreign Relations Committee which also asked that he be allowed to see her. He was turned down, but had returned to the United States determined to help the Bhutto women.

Benazir's letter to Peter Galbraith said, among other things, "Did they teach us that life could be full of such terrible dangers and tragedies.... Freedom and liberty, the essays we wrote on them, papers for our tutors, for grades, but did we know the value of those words which we bandied about, or how precious they are, as precious as the air we breathe, the water we drink."

Finally, the wedding celebration was over, and Benazir was taken back to jail. This time, she was taken to a smaller, darker cell. There, she would read, write, and think about her country and its future.

On December 11, 1981, the deputy superintendent came to Benazir's cell and told her to pack her belongings. She would be taken to Larkana the next morning under police escort. Strangely enough, Benazir was sad to leave the Karachi Central Jail. At least she knew what to expect there.

The next day she was driven to her family home, Al-Murtaza. She was told she would be free to use the telephone and have visitors. Her happiness at this news did not last long. The only visitors she could have were a few relatives. She was allowed no telephone calls, except to and from relatives. She tried to learn how to cook to make the long, dull days pass quickly.

Along with these difficulties came news that Nusrat Bhutto's health was not good. In fact, news that she had cancer had been leaked to reporters in London and other cities. This resulted in another campaign to "save the Bhutto ladies." Zia, however, did not want Nusrat to leave Pakistan. He directed her doctor to sign a report claiming that further medical treatment was not necessary. Risking his personal safety, Nusrat's physician refused to follow Zia's orders, as did all the doctors on the medical board.

On November 20, 1982, Nusrat was allowed to travel to West Germany and Switzerland for medical treatment. To say farewell to her mother, Benazir was driven under heavy military guard to the airport, and flown to Karachi after eleven months in Larkana.

Feeling lonely, Benazir parted from her mother at 70 Clifton. Instead of returning to Larkana, Benazir was placed under house arrest in Karachi for another fourteen months.

In December 1982, General Zia made an official visit to the United States to meet with President Ronald Reagan. There, the Senate Foreign Relations Committee challenged him with the reported abuse of political prisoners in Pakistan. When they demanded to know the location of Benazir Bhutto, he lost his temper and said, "I can tell you she lives in a better house than any senator and is allowed visitors and can use the telephone."

To challenge that statement, Peter Galbraith telephoned the Bhutto residence in Karachi and asked to speak to

Benazir. "You cannot speak to her. It is forbidden," was the answer. Even after identifying himself and saying he had President Zia's permission, the guards refused to let him speak to her.

Unaware of these efforts, Benazir began 1983 ill and tense. She began grinding her teeth at night, and woke to find her knuckles swollen. The problems with her ear returned, too, and would not go away. To try to ease the pain and isolation, she prayed daily to God.

Meanwhile, the Senate Foreign Relations Committee, under the constant pressure of Peter Galbraith, kept asking Pakistan about Benazir Bhutto's confinement. The committee personally asked Pakistan's foreign minister on his Washington visit about Bhutto's treatment. He was shocked by the facts they presented to him, and promised to investigate immediately.

Despite her physical problems, Benazir was encouraged by news that the Movement to Restore Democracy (MRD) was still resisting the military. Taking heart from this news, Benazir wrote encouraging letters to the group with her mother's name on them. She did not want to use her own name for fear she would be punished for taking part in illegal activities. She thought that her mother, now living in Europe, would be safe from any punishment.

By June 1983, the infection in Benazir's ear was constant. Her doctor told the authorities that Benazir needed special treatment in Europe. In December, the government granted her permission to go to Switzerland for surgery. When they gave her the news, Benazir could hardly believe it. She was afraid to show any emotion or excitement. Her feelings, after seven years, had become numb.

POLITICS IN EXILE

In January 1984, Benazir Bhutto stepped from the airplane onto the runway in Geneva, Switzerland. Her eyes, used to darkness from her years in prison, squinted in the blinding sunlight. Her mother was there to greet her and Sanam.

"Yesterday, I was a prisoner. Today, I am free with my mother and sister. We are together. We are all alive," Benazir said gratefully.

The reunion was a very happy one, interrupted by telephone calls from relatives and well-wishers. Benazir's brother Mir, who was living in Switzerland, came to see her with his little daughter, eighteen-month-old Fathi. Mir, now twenty-nine, was handsome and gentle. Her other brother, Shah, could not come from the south of France to meet her. The last time she had seen him, he had been eighteen years old. He was now twenty-five.

As much as Benazir wanted to stay close to her reunited family, she needed to go to London for medical treatment. She also wanted to continue her political opposition to Zia. This she could do in England. At that time, there were already 378,000 Pakistanis living in the country.

Sanam, who now lived in London with her husband, traveled with Benazir to London's Heath-row Airport. Word had spread among the Pakistani community of her arrival, and a large crowd awaited her. Strangers thought Benazir was a movie star. When they learned she was a political leader, they asked if she was going into exile.

"I was born in Pakistan and I'm going to die in Pakistan," she replied. To her fellow Pakistanis, she said, "I am not giving up on you. I will stay by your side until my last breath. The Bhuttos keep their promises."

For a short while, Benazir was a guest at her Aunt Behjat's apartment in London's Knightsbridge section. The telephone never stopped ringing, and visitors streamed through the apartment at all hours. But when a car, filled with Pakistani men, began following Benazir wherever she went, she became suspicious. Her aunt called Scotland Yard, the detective department of the London police. The car soon vanished from in front of the apartment building.

Benazir had difficulties adjusting to her freedom. A fear of crowds, and of being followed, bothered her. Even the closed-in feeling of the underground subway kept her above ground, using taxis for all her travel. Not wanting to disappoint the Pakistanis who looked to her as a strong figure, she kept these fears to herself.

Shortly after her arrival in London, Peter Galbraith arrived and met with Benazir. He had flown to Pakistan to try to see her, but found out she had already been released. He had not seen her since 1977, and noticed that she had a new self-confidence. They discussed the personal changes in their lives and those of their friends.

Peter tried to persuade Benazir to go to America and apply for a fellowship at Harvard. "My first obligation is to the party. In political terms, it makes more sense for me to be here, where the Pakistani community is larger," she replied.

Finally, in late January, Benazir underwent surgery on her ear. The doctors told her it would take nine months for her to recover. Nusrat Bhutto's health had greatly improved since she left Pakistan. She now came from Switzerland and rented an apartment in the London suburbs where she could help restore *her* daughter's health.

During these long months, Benazir developed a plan to wage a publicity campaign in the international press. She wanted to expose the cruel treatment of 40,000 political prisoners held in Pakistan. She began by providing specific information to Amnesty International, a worldwide organization that seeks to have political prisoners freed.

As a result of these efforts, the Carnegie Endowment for International Peace in Washington, D.C., invited Bhutto to speak in March 1984. With her girlhood friend Yasmin Niazi, she flew to the United States to speak for the Carnegie Endowment. She also visited senators and State Department officials. She asked for their public support in demanding the release of political prisoners in Pakistan.

In the Senate Foreign Relations Committee, they asked her if aid to Pakistan should be stopped. As much as Bhutto was opposed to Zia's policies, she answered by saying, "Cutting off aid will only create misunderstandings between our two countries. Both our countries would be better served if aid were linked to the restoration of human rights and democracy to Pakistan." The committee decided to continue aid to Pakistan.

Upon returning to England, Bhutto found an apartment to rent near Saint Paul's Cathedral. It had security guards, which reduced her fear of unwanted visitors, and let her check the people coming and going. The small apartment became the headquarters for the Pakistan People's Party (PPP) abroad.

Once again, Bhutto increased her efforts to save her country's political prisoners. Her first effort was to produce a news magazine in both Urdu and English. Benazir also traveled all over England and other parts of Europe, speaking to Pakistani groups. She slowly established a small, but growing, opposition to Zia.

Faced with this threat, Zia sentenced many prisoners to death. Benazir protested these executions by appealing to Elliot Abrams, the assistant secretary of state for human rights. She also spoke to members of Parliament.

United States government leaders, too, began to put pressure on Zia. They insisted he hold general elections in Pakistan, which he agreed to schedule for March 1985. But first, he announced a referendum for December 20, 1984. This would give the people of Pakistan an opportunity to say whether or not they wanted elections to be held. Zia told the Pakistanis that a vote for general elections would be a vote against Islam.

Through their news magazine and a secret organization in Pakistan and abroad, Benazir Bhutto and the PPP attempted to inform voters about the referendum. They urged people to boycott the vote. The Manchester *Guardian,* a London newspaper, later reported that only 10 percent of Pakistanis had voted. The government, however, claimed 64 percent had voted.

After the referendum, general elections were scheduled for March. PPP leaders suggested that Benazir Bhutto return to Pakistan to challenge Zia. The suggestion was soon dismissed when Benazir learned that her Karachi home was surrounded by the army. A warrant for the arrest of Nusrat and Benazir had been issued.

The March election was held, and Zia won—although the turnout was again very low. Zia then announced that he would change his government from a military to a civilian government.

Sadly, the execution of political prisoners continued. Frustrated, Benazir Bhutto spoke out publicly. She spoke at Harvard in 1985, addressing the Council on Foreign Relations. She also delivered a speech to the members of the European Parliament in Strasbourg.

At Strasbourg, she said, "When the conscience of the world is justly aroused against apartheid and against human rights violations... then that conscience ought not to close its eyes to the murder by military courts which takes place in a country which receives... aid from the West itself." Following this speech, more than 54 prisoners in Lahore were sentenced to death.

In mid-1985, Benazir felt she needed a break from the constant pressures of politics. She arranged a vacation with members of her family in the south of France.

After her plane landed in Cannes, Benazir looked around for someone to meet her. There was no one. Suddenly, her brother Shah jumped out from behind a pillar to surprise her. The other family members came out from their hiding places, too. Benazir was very happy to see her youngest brother.

Shah had always had a special fondness for Benazir. He had written to her frequently when she had first left home to go to Harvard. Later, Alt Bhutto had sent Shah away to military school. He thought his mischievous young son needed to learn some discipline. For Shah, it was a very unhappy experience. He had pleaded with his mother to let him return to Islamabad and attend the International

School there. She had finally agreed. Not only did Shah like to play pranks, he was very generous. If someone asked him for his coat, he would give it away to them.

After Mir and Shah had escaped to Afghanistan at the time of the coup, they met and married sisters. Mir and Fauzia had eventually moved to Switzerland. Shah and his wife, Rehana, had a daughter named Sassi and were now living in Cannes. Unfortunately, Shah's marriage was not a happy one, and the couple only stayed together for the sake of their daughter.

Knowing this, Benazir was not surprised when Shah told her he intended to divorce his wife. Nevertheless, Benazir pleaded with him to make every effort to remain together. She also tried to befriend Rehana during her month-long stay in Cannes, but found the other woman to be somewhat unfriendly.

On the morning Shah had planned to take Benazir to Nice, in southern France, the two Bhutto women received a disturbing phone call from Rehana. Something was wrong with Shah, she told them. He had taken poison.

What followed seemed a nightmare to Benazir. When she and Nusrat arrived at Shah's apartment, they found him dead on the living room floor. Although the official explanation was suicide, many people suspected a political murder.

Against the advice of friends and relatives, Benazir decided in August 1985 to take the body of her brother back to the family grave in Larkana, Pakistan. The Pakistani military leaders were not pleased with this decision, yet they could not stop the burial. Worldwide publicity and pressure would be bad for the current government.

The mourners crowded into Larkana and Karachi. Once again, the government detained Benazir. But this time, the U.S. State Department protested. In an official statement, a spokesperson said, "Pakistan has taken encouraging steps toward... constitutional government.... Putting Ms. Bhutto under house arrest would appear... inconsistent with this process."

Meanwhile, Rehana had been arrested in connection with Shah's death, and Benazir had been asked to appear in court. In November, she was allowed to leave Pakistan to testify in Nice, France. Due to the suspicions against Rehana, Mir and Fauzia had separated.

Eventually, Sassi, Shah's daughter, was sent to live with grandparents in the United States. To this day, the Bhuttos do not know where she is. They refuse to give up hope, though, because Sassi's name means, "one who crosses the deserts and mountains to find the family who loves her."

"Difficulty is a part of everyday life," says Benazir Bhutto when remembering this period of her life. "I took my father for granted and lost him. My brother was so young when he died—and in a safe place like France. Suddenly, when those who are closest to you are gone, you think of all those unspoken words. We don't appreciate our mothers and fathers, and the gift they are to you."

9

Work for Democracy

Toward the end of 1985, Bhutto traveled throughout Europe to speak to groups of Pakistanis. She inspired them with the promise of restoring democracy in Pakistan. During one of these rallies, she heard that martial law had been lifted.

Bhutto was immediately suspicious. Her past experience with General Zia made her doubt his promises. She learned that before the civilian government took office, many organizers in the opposition party were arrested and sentenced to long jail terms. In this way, Zima removed the "troublemakers."

Despite Zia's step to move away from military rule, Benazir reminded everyone that democracy had all but disappeared since Ali Bhutto's death. Crime and corruption (dishonesty), especially in the cities, had risen. Since 1979, when the Soviet Union had invaded Afghanistan, refugees from that country had been fleeing to Pakistan. Money and weapons, coming from the United States to help the Afghan fighters and refugees, found their way into the Pakistani black market. This meant those guns and rifles were for sale in the public bazaars, or marketplaces, of Pakistan. The drug problem, too, was beyond control.

Farmers used their fields to grow poppies (used in making heroin) instead of food crops.

Also during his rule, Zia had used some of the more extreme ideas of the Islamic religion to support his political policies. One of these was to limit the freedom of women. *Mullahs,* Muslim religious leaders, insisted that all women in Pakistan wear the traditional Pakistani dress in public at all times. Also, if a woman were even suspected of being unfaithful to her husband, she could be jailed and stoned to death. By 1989, most of the prisoners in the Karachi Central Jail were women.

Zia, though, did not expect the behavior that resulted from these harsh religious laws. Violence increased throughout the country, not only men against women, but province against province, and man against man. No one liked the religious tax placed on personal income, either.

Because of the violent conditions growing within Pakistan, Benazir Bhutto met with fellow party leaders in her London apartment. They discussed her future, as well as Pakistan's future.

In January 1986, Benazir made an announcement. "I'm going home," she told members of the PPP. Instead of rejecting this decision, they agreed with her. Most felt it was time she went back. Although her personal safety would be at risk, events around the world pointed toward a spread of democracy. Dictators had been overthrown in Haiti and the Philippines, and many felt it was Pakistan's turn.

In London, the PPP leaders carefully planned Bhutto's trip. As they decided upon their strategy, rumors spread about her possible return. The Bhuttos received messages telling her not to return, that she would be killed. People telephoned in the middle of the night, threatening to stop her.

Bhutto refused to be frightened by these threats. She flew to the United States for discussions with American senators and representatives of the Democratic party in

Congress. She believed that their public support would insure her safety and protection.

Yet her greatest security would be the international media. They were attracted to the story of a beautiful young woman leading her followers to freedom. Reporters and television cameras covered and publicized her every move, from Washington, to London, to Mecca, where Muslims make a spiritual pilgrimage. At Mecca, Bhutto's prayers prepared her for the challenge ahead.

Finally, a date was chosen for her arrival in Lahore. Although confident about her decision, Benazir was worried. Would her people welcome her, or would they be afraid of the police? She feared that they might be angry with her, or would not care about her return.

As the airplane circled for its landing at dawn, Benazir and her colleagues stared out the windows in surprise. The runway and surrounding areas of the airport were thick with the bobbing heads of people. Over the loudspeaker, the pilot said, "We welcome Miss Benazir Bhutto back to Pakistan." From the air controllers, the pilot received word that a million people were on the ground to greet Benazir Bhutto.

Benazir was shocked at the huge crowd awaiting her. When her feet finally touched the land of her birth, she knew she was where she belonged. The sweet smell of jasmine in the air brought back familiar memories. For a brief moment, she felt a touch of sadness for her father. These memories were soon set aside, however, in the crush of the crowd. The people greeted her with chants of "Live, live, Bhutto live!" and "Benazir has come, revolution has come!"

Benazir was quickly pushed onto the deck of a truck. She stood on a platform, waving to the masses of people. From there, they would be able to see her on the way to the Minar-i-Pakistan monument. This monument had special meaning for Benazir. Her father had authorized it to be built as a symbol of Pakistan's birth. Although only minutes away from the airport normally, it took ten hours to reach because the crowd swelled to 3 million.

Showers of rose petals and balloons filled the air, adding to the festive and noisy atmosphere. By the time the truck reached the monument, it was dusk. Benazir stepped onto the specially erected stage to the sound of cheers.

The crowd quieted as she began to speak. "Here and now," she told the waiting Pakistanis, "I vow I will make every sacrifice to secure people's rights. Do you want freedom? Do you want democracy? Do you want a revolution?" Each time, the people responded with a loud "yes."

"I put an end to revenge. I don't have any such feelings in my heart. I want to build Pakistan," she continued. The crowd responded by saying, "Zia must go."

There were threatening incidents during her stay in Lahore. Everywhere Bhutto went, she spoke of her democratic dream for Pakistan. "People think I am weak because I am a woman. Do they know I am a Muslim woman, and that the Muslim women have a heritage to be proud of?" she asked.

Bhutto left her mark throughout Pakistan. In the northern Punjab province, the police presented her with a restraining order. Thinking she would ignore it, they were ready to arrest her. Instead, she returned to Karachi, and her home at 70 Clifton.

There, she prepared to celebrate Pakistan's Independence Day on August 14, 1986, with the MRD and PPP. The foreign press arrived, including her Harvard classmate, Anne Fadiman.

On Independence day, Fadiman recorded the events of Bhutto's day. She described Bhutto's morning prayer within the doors of her home, and the dusty sport stadium in Lyari, where 10,000 people waited for Bhutto's arrival.

Inside the stadium, the people chanted, "We'll beat them; we'll die; but we'll bring Benazir," over and over again.

Before Bhutto could reach the place from where she would speak, though, the police sprayed the air with tear gas. As they followed her van and came closer, she escaped to a cab. It took her home while the police were led on a false trail by a friend wearing her dupatta.

Not long after this, the police arrested Bhutto and placed her in solitary confinement in Landhi Borstal Jail on the outskirts of Karachi; the Central Jail was full of political prisoners. There she stayed until she was freed in September. Although free, there were now assassination attempts on Bhutto's life. To be safe, she often made three different plans for every trip to keep her enemies guessing. To Benazir, it seemed as if the struggle had just begun.

SERVING THE NATION

In the summer of 1987, Benazir Bhutto made an announcement that pleased Zia's government, and worried some or her supporters. She planned to marry. Because of this, Zia decided to hold elections one year earlier than scheduled. He hoped the people would think her marriage would force her out of politics.

Although Bhutto was not a traditional Pakistani woman, she had agreed to an arranged marriage. This was due partly to the unusual set of circumstances in her public life. She explained to her Radcliffe classmate, Anne Fadiman. "For me, the choice was not between a love marriage and an arranged marriage, but between an arranged marriage and no marriage. It simply would not be possible for me to have a date or get to know a man the way you could. Even the hint of a relationship would have been used by my opponents to destroy me politically."

Nusrat Bhutto had been trying to arrange a marriage for her daughter since Benazir's graduation from Radcliffe. Again and again, Benazir resisted the idea. After her father's death, marriage was definitely set aside. When she was imprisoned, detained, and exiled to England, marriage could not even be considered. Also, Benazir wondered if a man could live her kind of life—the constant travel and political meetings. The Pakistani people would have to come first, not a husband.

In addition, her time in prison had made her frightened of sudden noises, and very nervous around people—even her family. When her mother had pressed her on the subject of an arranged marriage, Bhutto had said, "I have to find myself before I am ready to marry. I have to find a relative calm. I need time to recover."

Despite all these protests, a single woman in a Muslim country could have a very difficult time. Realizing this, Nusrat Bhutto, an untraditional Muslim woman herself, had begun searching for a suitable husband for Benazir in 1985. With the help of Benazir's aunts, they chose a young man of Benazir's age. He came from the Sindh Province, too, and was from a wealthy, landowning family. Asif Ali Zardari had studied at the London Centre of Economic and Political Studies and was very athletic, especially as a polo player. Asif had been brought to Benazir's aunt's house for inspection. Nusrat approved. But before she could tell Benazir, Shah had died. With this tragic news, marriage was once again out of the question.

In February 1987, Bhutto flew to England to appear on a television panel discussion about Afghanistan. Once there, the subject of marriage came up again. Bhutto's aunt and mother continued to press her about meeting Asif. His stepmother had even come to London to speak to the Bhutto women about him.

Still afraid of taking this step, Bhutto pleaded with her mother, asking to wait until June to make a decision. But back in Karachi, Asifs stepmother approached Benazir directly at a meeting at the 70 Clifton home.

"My politics are a commitment to freedom and the meaning of life," Benazir told the woman. "How would a man feel, knowing that his wife's life does not revolve around him?"

"My dear," the stepmother replied, "Asif is a very confident young man. He knows what he is in for."

In July 1987, Bhutto returned to London. At a brief social meeting in the living room of her aunt's apartment, surrounded by relatives, she met Asif Zardari. Although they did not speak directly to each other, the next day Asif sent Benazir roses. Mangoes and candy arrived the following day.

Yet Benazir was still unsure, and would not give her mother an answer. She made her decision a few days later. At a social gathering, Benazir was stung by a bee. Asif insisted he drive her to the hospital. She was impressed with his caring, his sense of humor, and with his generous nature—many of the qualities her brothers had.

Within seven days of their arranged meeting, Benazir agreed to become engaged to Asif Ali Zardari. In December 1987, the Bhutto-Zardari wedding took place before two hundred guests at 70 Clifton. A ceremony was also held before thousands at the Lyari stadium, where the crowds cheered for the newly married couple.

A number of Muslim customs were bypassed for their marriage. The rule requiring two weeks of isolation for a bride-to-be was ignored because of Bhutto's work schedule. Also, instead of the seven sets of jewelry traditionally given to the bride from the groom, she preferred to receive two simple sets. She also decided to keep her father's name instead of taking her husband's.

The marriage conditions, traditionally chanted by family and friends, were vastly different from the typical vows. Asif had to agree to look after any children, and to allow his wife to go to jail for the sake of her beliefs. "You must agree that Benazir will serve the nation," the Bhutto family sang.

"That is all right with me, for I will serve the nation by serving my wife," Asif replied.

At the age of thirty-four, Benazir had entered a warm

and understanding marriage that the Muslim world could approve of. But contrary to what Zia's government thought, she was not giving up politics. She promised to continue her political fight against Zia's government.

At the end of May 1988, Zia made a surprise move. He dissolved Parliament and called for free elections in ninety days. The members of the PPP were overjoyed, but Bhutto was suspicious. This had happened too many times before. She thought there must be some political reason for him to make such a move.

Sanam offered a possible reason for Zia's action. Zia's announcement followed another announcement made by Benazir and Asif: they were expecting their first child in September. Sanam guessed that Zia expected Bhutto to stay at home and not campaign. He might have also believed that her recent marriage and new baby would turn voters against her.

In preparing for the upcoming elections, Zia passed even stricter laws. The first was to declare *Shariah,* or Islamic law, as the supreme law of the land. According to Shariah, an ordinary citizen could take any law to the high courts and call it un-Islamic. In this way, Zia hoped someone would challenge the right of women to run for high government offices. This could make it unlawful for Bhutto to be a leading candidate. However, the constitution of 1973 made it legal for women to enter elections, so Zia's plan failed.

Zia's next action was to make all nine political parties register with the government. This would give him the power to decide which parties could participate in the elections. Fortunately, the PPP presented a strong case before the Supreme Court against the government and won. The court agreed that Zia's action was illegal according to the constitution.

An unexpected accident in the summer of 1988 changed the course of events for Pakistan and for Bhutto. On August 17, Bhutto learned that General Zia's plane had crashed after take-off in a Punjabi town. All thirty passengers were said to be dead, including General Zia and the United States ambassador to Pakistan.

Bhutto was stunned by the thought that eleven years of dictatorship might finally be over. She could not be completely happy, though. She knew that martial law could be declared. To her relief, Pakistan's former chairman of the senate took over as president, and announced that the elections would be held as scheduled.

The shocking news of Zia's death led to many rumors. Some viewed the crash as an act of God, while others thought someone might have tampered with the aircraft. Still others believed that India had fired a missile and downed the plane, or that the Soviet's had sought revenge for Zia's support of the Afghan rebels. Although the facts were never fully uncovered, most experts agreed it was a mechanical failure in the plane.

Although Zia was no longer a threat to her, Bhutto continued to campaign. Nearly 18,000 candidates had registered for 700 national and provincial government seats. With 80 percent of the population expected to vote, Bhutto could not afford to waste time.

Her activities were interrupted on September 21, 1988, when her son Bilawal, meaning, "one without equal," was born. From the beginning, Asif treasured his son, saying "He looks just like me." Benazir was happy that her son would have the same father's love she had felt from Alt Bhutto.

Within five days of Bilawal's birth, Bhutto was back at work. Zia's death had not stopped the threats and violence aimed at Bhutto and the PPP. But wherever she went, large, enthusiastic crowds greeted her.

When the polls were closed on November 16, 1988, the PPP had won major political contests in all four provinces, including 92 seats in the National Assembly. On December 1, Benazir Bhutto was declared prime minister of Pakistan.

Not only was she the first woman to lead a Muslim nation, but at thirty-five years of age, she was one of the youngest heads of state in the world.

In the forty-one years since Pakistan's creation, there had only been one democratic, free election—her father's in 1977. Now, for the second time in history, a Bhutto was attempting to bring democracy to Pakistan.

10

The New Leader

Following the election, the streets of Pakistan were filled with people celebrating their new leader. Posters and cardboard cut-outs of her appeared on walls or in the middle of traffic circles. Every major city in Pakistan was ablaze with color and a carnival-like atmosphere.

Bhutto had little time to celebrate. She began the huge task of restoring democracy to her nation and healing the wounds of dictatorship. She and her family moved from Asif's house in Karachi to the capital, Islamabad.

The new prime minister was faced with many problems. Dealing with the military was one of her most difficult tasks. Military leaders had been in power for most of Pakistan's four decades, especially during Zia's eleven-year reign. Through out this period, the armed forces had become more and more corrupt, or dishonest. Some sources claimed this was caused by low wages. If people offered the soldiers money for favors, many of them accepted. This resulted in widespread bribery.

From the time Bhutto became prime minister, the military kept a careful watch on her policies. They were concerned about whether or not she would cut their budget. According to Pakistani newspapers, military officials were also waiting to see whether a civilian government could maintain law and order without them.

Pakistan's relationship with Afghanistan was another difficult issue for Bhutto. While the Soviets still occupied Afghanistan, Pakistan would not recognize the Afghan government. Once the Soviet army left in 1988, however, this policy had to change. During the ten-year Soviet occupation, an unofficial government made up of Afghan refugees had been formed in Peshawar, Pakistan, near the border with Afghanistan. Pakistan, under Zia's rule, had recognized this group as the real, democratic government of Afghanistan.

Yet when the Soviets pulled out of Afghanistan in 1988, they left behind their own appointed leaders. In order to keep peace, Bhutto now had to deal with both the existing government in Kabul, the capital of Afghanistan, and the unofficial one in Peshawar. Until Afghanistan holds free elections, Butte's dealings with that country require great patience and diplomacy.

As a result of the Afghan war, drug trafficking in Pakistan has increased. Since the beginning of the war, an estimated 700,000 Pakistanis have become heroin addicts. To fight this problem, Bhutto has encouraged the growers of poppy seeds—which are used in making heroin—to plow up their fields and plant orchards and onions instead. These bring as much profit as the poppies.

Many observers think that Bhutto may be able to resolve the problems with Afghanistan and drugs. Pakistan's relationship with India, though, continues to be a difficult issue.

After she took office, Bhutto and India's Prime Minister Rajiv Gandhi tried to solve the problems between Pakistan and India. In addition to some cultural exchanges, both leaders had agreed not to use nuclear force against each other. Since the two countries have always been rivals, Bhutto was criticized for making these agreements. Many critics said that she had given in to India, Gandhi was defeated in 1989, however. With that country's new leadership, the future relationship between the two neighbors remains uncertain.

Since her election, Bhutto has tried to reform the education system. At the present time, nearly 74 percent of Pakistanis cannot read or write. Bhutto hopes to change this. With her new minister of state for education, Shahnaz Wazir Alt, Bhutto is trying to offer more Pakistanis an education.

There is some resistance to these efforts, however, among Muslim men and religious leaders who do not want girls or women to go to school. Also, rural families often need their oldest children to stay home and look after the younger ones, or to work to help support the family.

Bhutto has had more success in helping older children. She has started a technical training program for young people who are educated, but cannot find jobs. Critics, however, say she should have done this much sooner after her election.

In order to provide more jobs for all Pakistanis, Bhutto has been working to improve the country's economy. New plans to develop Pakistan's manufacturing and agricultural industries have been designed. Also, to encourage investment in the country, Bhutto wants to make it easier for new private companies to get started. She has recommended lowering taxes for them and decreasing the time it takes to get permits.

Pakistan has just re-entered the British Commonwealth, an organization of nations who have promised to cooperate with Great Britain. This gives it many opportunities to increase its fortunes by lowering the cost of trading with Great Britain and other European countries. Also, in May 1990, the country will experiment with privatization—allowing publicly owned companies to become privately owned.

The pressures on Benazir Bhutto as prime minister, and

as a young woman with a growing family, are enormous. As a result, the time she spends with her family is valued. When she travels to other countries for conferences and meetings, Asif and Bilawal often go with her. Sometimes, Bilawal rides with her to work in the mornings. He might also be there to greet her at the end of the day. Since she is gone for most of the day, this is a private time when they can be together.

Bhutto's work day is a long one. She usually reaches her office at the General Secretariat at 8:00 A.M. each morning. The office is large and square, paneled in wood and carpeted in soft gray with matching gray curtains. Two sofas face each other, separated by a long table filled with magazines, newspapers, and an appointment book. The Pakistani and PPP flags hang behind her desk of simply carved, dark wood. Chests stand against the walls, and the only personal touch is a crystal vase filled with fresh flowers.

Bhutto's clothes are made up of a variety of shalwar kamiz in bright colors. Her dupatta is usually white, but, on occasion, she wears a yellow one. Tall and slender, Bhutto's skin is fair and her eyes a deep brown. She looks directly at the person with whom she is talking, and offers a firm handshake.

As soon as Bhutto arrives each day, her military secretary hands her a schedule of appointments. Throughout the day, two male attendants stand on either side of her office door. They wear tan shalwar kamiz with bright red vests and hats. The attendants serve the visitors and act as messengers and guards. Although Bhutto's appointments finish at 5:00 P.M., the receptions, policy meetings, and visiting diplomats and heads of state usually extend her day to fourteen and sometimes sixteen hours.

"I used to spend sixteen hours a day in a jeep with the heat beating down on me," Bhutto recalls. "We would sleep for a few hours and get up again. I was never tired. Now I work from eight to five, and 1 go home tired."

After a long day, Bhutto returns to the prime minister's residence, high on a sloping hill, ten minutes away from her office. The house, with a grand view of Islamabad, once belonged to the chief minister of Sindh. Bhutto felt it suited the needs of her family better than the official residence in Rawalpindi.

In addition to the many duties she has in Pakistan, Bhutto frequently visits other countries to deliver speeches. In June 1989, she was invited to the United States to speak before a joint session of Congress. In her Pakistani national dress and white chiffon scarf, her words about Pakistan's newfound freedom filled the chamber. The members applauded this new leader of Pakistan.

"My friends, freedom is not an end," Bhutto declared. "Freedom is a beginning. Let us stand together now as the people of Pakistan strive to give meaning to their newfound freedom. Come with us toward a tomorrow better than all the yesterdays we knew. History, the rush of events, perhaps even destiny, has brought me here today...."

As the members listened attentively, Bhutto continued. "As a representative of the young, let me be viewed as one of the new generation of leaders, unshackled by the constraints and irrational hatreds of the past. As a representative of women, let my message be, 'Yes, you can.' And as a believer in Islam... let my message be about a compassionate and tolerant religion, teaching hard work and family values under a merciful God."

After her appearance before Congress, Benazir and Asif were honored at a White House dinner. During her visit, President George Bush promised to give $4.2 billion in financial aid to Pakistan over the course of six years. Bush also said the United States would supply Pakistan with 60 fighter bombers and an additional $600 million for economic and military aid. In return, Bhutto had to promise she would not let her country become a nuclear power.

Early in 1990, however, Bhutto made an agreement with

China in which that country agreed to build a nuclear power station for Pakistan. Although Bhutto denied any intentions of using the power for defensive weapons, doubts have been expressed by India and other countries.

While still in Washington, D.C., in 1989, Benazir Bhutto met with fifteen of her friends from Harvard. According to her Harvard roommate, Yolanda Kodrzycki Henderson, "The meeting at Blair House was special. We talked as friends. She had a sense of what the ordinary people of Pakistan want. Despite her wealth, I've seen her among rural people, and she knows and understands what their aspirations [hopes] are.... She is very adaptable, as she was at Radcliffe when she first arrived at the age of sixteen."

From the nation's capital, Prime Minister Bhutto traveled to Cambridge, Massachusetts. There, she gave the commencement address at Harvard University to the 1989 graduating class. For her, it was a sentimental time. In the soft rain, she spoke mainly about freedom and democracy, and how Pakistan had fought for it.

In a 1989 interview, Bhutto was asked for her advice to young people, and to her own children. The prime minister said she hoped they would "learn to stand on their own two feet...to have confidence in themselves... and to be patient. People ruin their chances by impatience and by wanting too much too soon. I would want them to be a good sport and know that they will win some and lose some."

When Bhutto returned from the United States after her visit, she continued to face growing opposition. Her critics accused her of not making changes fast enough. Others said she was using the Bhutto name to get what she wanted. They also accused Asif of making business deals for the government and taking 10 percent of each deal. Angered, Bhutto defended her husband and demanded evidence to back up these accusations.

One of the prime minister's closest and most respected

associates has said, "It is very difficult for her to get things done because she has to pay attention to the political parties and pressures that would try to unseat her.... She does not know whom to trust—even those closest to her. She is very bright—far more intelligent than any around her. I would not like to confront the problems facing her, such as a 3 percent population increase annually, but she has patience."

One of the most frustrating problems facing Bhutto now is the issue of women's rights. For years, Pakistani women have had far fewer rights than women in many other nations. One of Bhutto's goals is to achieve equal rights for Pakistani women. Her chief political rivals, however, as well as many Pakistani men, are against any change in current laws. These opponents criticize her of wanting to make too many changes. Others accuse her of moving too slowly.

Fortunately, Bhutto has learned how to deal with criticism by the press and by her government. "To cope with criticism," she said, "I don't start my day by reading newspapers. My press secretary presents me with a written summary. I get through what I have to do. By evening, I'm thick-skinned. Actually, I don't mind criticism. I know I'm not an angel. The press is a fact of life."

In November 1989, the criticism against Bhutto reached a high point. The National Assembly decided to take a vote of "no confidence" against the prime minister and the PPP. If a majority of National Assembly members had voted against her, a new national election would have been called. But Bhutto and the PPP survived this election by twelve votes and remained in power.

After the election, Bhutto's cabinet resigned, allowing her to select new members. Some came from political parties other than the PPP. Advisers felt this would help to increase her popularity.

The move from critic to leader has not been easy for Bhutto. Her main political rival is Nawaz Sharif, the chief minister of Punjab province. He has criticized the prime minister for failing to be an effective leader, wasting opportunities, and for not passing any major new laws. Bhutto also faces opposition from President Ghulam Ishaq Khan. They have not had a good relationship, due in part to the president's former association with General Zia.

In spite of these political troubles, Benazir Bhutto is greatly admired by most Pakistanis and by many world leaders. Before Benazir had completed her first year in office, Nusrat Bhutto—now Benazir's senior minister—traveled to the United States. There, she accepted the Averrell W. Harri-man Award for her daughter's role in restoring democracy to Pakistan.

"The principle of humanity should be promoted, and we should reach out to each other because we are all the creatures of God," Benazir Bhutto has said. She tries to promote the principles of humanity—being respectful to each other— in her own life. Although she was imprisoned by her opponents for nearly ten years, she holds no bitterness toward them.

"The last words my father said to me from his jail in Rawalpindi were, 'I don't want you to be bitter.' Every time I would feel bitter, I would think of this. I didn't want to fail him." Benazir hopes to pass on these beliefs to her son, Bilawal, and to her daughter, Bakhatawar, who was born January 25, 1990. In the Sindhi language, Bakhatawar means "full of hope."

To the world, Benazir Bhutto has become a symbol of freedom. To Pakistanis, she has become a hope for a better future. The prime minister has her own vision for Pakistan: "I would like Pakistan to be at peace with its neighbors. I would like it to be stable and independent. I would like Pakistan to emerge out of the darkness of illiteracy and have the world judge our country on its talents and merits. I would like to see equal opportunities for men and women, and have other Asian countries point to Pakistan and say, 'If Pakistan can break through illiteracy, so can we.'"

It is too early to tell if Bhutto's vision for the struggling nation of Pakistan will be achieved. Yet, whether or not she reaches her goals, her belief in her abilities, and in the future of her country, will not falter. "When you believe," the young prime minister states, "then there is no mountain high enough to scale. That is my message to the youth of America, to its women, and to its people."

11

Prime Minister of Pakistan

On December 2, 1988, Benazir Bhutto was sworn in as the prime minister of Pakistan, setting many firsts. She was the first woman to lead a modern Muslim nation. She was the first person to lead Pakistan through totally open and free elections. And she became the youngest current head of state in the world. Many people throughout the country were jubilant as she assumed her position as the duly elected leader of Pakistan. Ironically, this was the first paying job Benazir Bhutto had ever held.

The people of Pakistan truly had reason to celebrate. The swearing-in of Benazir Bhutto heralded a new era for Pakistan. But there was also reason for concern: Benazir Bhutto and the Pakistan People's Party would have to depend on a coalition of independent and lesser party assembly members to keep the government together. Most threatening of all were the conditions within the country. Benazir Bhutto was faced with a number of problems, all demanding attention. On the eve other taking office, Pakistan was on the brink of bankruptcy. The International Monetary Fund was demanding certain concessions from Pakistan in exchange for the loans needed to get the country out of its current crisis. To placate the military, Benazir Bhutto had assured them that she would not tamper with military spending which was chewing up between 40 and 60 percent of Pakistan's budget. She had promised her supporters that she would work for improvements in the area of social reform and services. Unfortunately, she was faced with a budget in which the percentage of expenditure for social services was among the lowest in the world. Health care, housing, land reform, education, civil rights, and freedom of the press were all areas that cried out from eleven years of neglect by the military dictatorship of General Zia.

It was also up to Benazir Bhutto to deal with the drug problems within Pakistan and the bands of drug smugglers that had expanded during the Zia years. Speaking several days after her swearing-in, Prime Minister Bhutto stated that drugs were the number one problem in Pakistan. She also had to keep a lid on the ethnic violence that had always plagued the country and had been exceptionally bad in the last years that General Zia was in power. As part of the ethnic problem, she also had to somehow solve the problems created by three million Afghan refugees living in Pakistan, mostly along the Afghan-Pakistan border.

Internationally, Benazir Bhutto was also walking a thin line. The United States expected her support in its ongoing policy of aiding the Afghan rebels. The United States also wanted assurances that she would not pursue the Pakistani nuclear weapon program that had been started by her father and continued in secret by General Zia. The long-standing tensions between India and Pakistan were a perennial problem. The two countries had gone to war with each other three times since 1947.

To keep all the factions and problems within and outside Pakistan from tearing down the fragile democratic government, Benazir Bhutto had to prove that she could be as successful leading a country as she had been in leading the opposition. Her charismatic appeal to the people would have to be accompanied by a pragmatic ability to manage a country of 107 million people on a day-to-day basis. Many thought the task was beyond the ability of anyone.

One member of the opposition, Ms. Abida Hussein, said on the television news show 60 Minutes that "if Benazir Bhutto had a perfect head, perfect heart, and a perfect soul she'd probably still fail."

In her first speech as prime minister, Benazir Bhutto said, "We will choose the path of love. We will eradicate hunger and poverty. We will provide shelter for the homeless. We will provide employment for the unemployed. We will educate the illiterates." She went on to promise that women will be given full partnership in Pakistan. One of her first official acts was the freeing of one thousand prisoners still in General Zia's jails. Most of those freed were political prisoners. She then lifted curbs on student and labor unions that had been instituted during the days of martial law. One journalist likened the mood in Pakistan to the "Camelot" atmosphere of the Kennedy White House in the early 1960s.

The people of Pakistan basked in the newfound openness of the government of Benazir Bhutto. For the first time in eleven years they could openly talk politics. Even the opposition leaders were granted time on government-run television to criticize Benazir Bhutto and her government. This was a right that not even her father had granted his opposition. One Western journalist who had lived in Pakistan and had been expelled by the government in 1982, returned in December 1988. He found Pakistan a radically different place. People were open and willing to talk. The fear that had gripped the country under martial law had vanished.

The next order of business for the government was electing a president. Under the Pakistan constitution, the presidency is primarily a ceremonial position with the real power of the government resting with the prime minister. Acting President Ishaq Khan was the only serious candidate. He received the backing of both the Pakistan People's Party and the Islamic Democratic Alliance. When the election was held, he won 78 percent of the vote.

The Pakistani constitution also required that a new government undergo a vote of confidence in the National

Assembly within the first sixty days after taking office. On December 12, 1988, Prime Minister Bhutto put herself and her party up to the vote. They received 148 votes in favor of their government and only 55 no-confidence votes.

Benazir Bhutto was quickly thrust into the international spotlight as well. Her long struggle against General Zia, her imprisonments and exile gave her victory a fairy-tale quality that captured the imagination of the world press. She appeared on the cover of magazines throughout the world.

The scheduled three-day summit of the South Asian Association for Regional Cooperation (SAARC) December 29-31, 1988, would be Benazir Bhutto's first opportunity to interact with her fellow leaders of the neighboring South Asian states. Foremost among these would be Rajiv Gandhi, the prime minister of India. He would be the first Indian prime minister to visit Pakistan since his grandfather, Jawaharlal Nehru, visited in 1960. Gandhi's cooperation in reducing tensions between Pakistan and India would be very helpful to both leaders.

The results of the SAARC conference were considered a success for Benazir Bhutto. India and Pakistan signed a bilateral agreement stating that neither would attack the other's nuclear power installations. The conference as a whole reached agreement on cooperation and the sharing of intelligence in the ongoing fight against the drug trade in the area. The participants also reached a consensus on a number of issues that had to be dealt with during the next decade. The plan, called SAARC 2000, addresses many of the social ills that the 1.1 billion people of South Asia face.

The first few months of 1989 were marked by a lack of action on the part of the Bhutto government. Benazir Bhutto and the Pakistan People's Party had failed to present a single piece of legislation. Benazir Bhutto had done everything she could that did not cost money: freeing prisoners, lifting the ban on unions, permitting freedom of the press. Yet she was unable to come up with funding for any new programs. Her hands were tied by the concessions that had been made to the International Monetary Fund to get $800 million in loans. Despite the lack of action, her popularity among the people remained solid. Benazir Bhutto was maintaining the delicate balance within the country, trying to placate as many groups as possible. It seemed that the easiest way to do that was to do very little.

Prime Minister Bhutto's attempts at maintaining a balance among the factions in Pakistan met with mixed results. As in all political situations, each faction had its own ideas about how things should be done. The two most serious opposition factions were the religious fundamentalists and the provincial government of the Punjab led by Nawaz Sherif and the Islamic Democratic Alliance. Both tested the ability of the prime minister to weather political storms.

The most conservative among the religious leaders went so far as to claim that a woman, under Islamic law, was ineligible to lead a country. They called for the immediate removal of Prime Minister Bhutto. The Prime Minister met the challenge head on declaring that Islam is a religion, not a government. She also went on to state that she would do everything in her power to see that the women of Pakistan got equal rights under the law.

The challenge from Nawaz Sherif, who was seen by many as in league with the conservative religious leaders, was in many ways more serious. As the head of the provincial government of the Punjab, Nawaz Sherif controlled the largest, most populous, and wealthiest part of Pakistan. The Punjab was also the home of the majority of the military. General Zia was from the Punjab and the strongest remaining supporters for what he stood for, Nawaz Sherif among them, were to be found in the Punjab. Prime Minister Bhutto and the Pakistan People's Party members in the provincial assembly tried to unseat Sherif and his Alliance Party but were outmaneuvered. As they were still recruiting votes for a no-confidence vote, Sherif caught them unprepared with a confidence vote which he won.

Despite the battles with Sherif and the religious right wing. Prime Minister Bhutto retained much of her popularity. Many Pakistanis were relieved by her secularization of government. They also enjoyed the apparent renaissance that was beginning in the arts in Pakistan. Early in 1989 a One-hour television gala featured the singing and dancing of the brother and sister team of Mazia and Zohaib. The religious conservatives dubbed the show un-Islamic and unsuccessfully tried to have the performers punished. The majority of the Pakistani population sighed a collective sigh of relief to have entertainment on the state-owned TV. The permissiveness of Prime Minister Bhutto's new government spawned other artistic endeavors as well.

In April 1989 it was announced that Prime Minister Bhutto would make an official visit to the United States in June of that year. The agenda for the visit would be one of discussing the situation in Afghanistan with President Bush. Prime Minister Bhutto would also address the United States Congress in an attempt to strengthen support for continued aid to Pakistan. After completing her official duties in Washington, Prime Minister Bhutto would be the commencement speaker at Harvard University.

As the first official state visit of the Bush presidency, Prime Minister Bhutto was treated lavishly when she arrived in Washington on June 6, 1989. Just prior to her arrival, the White House announced that President Bush would recommend that the United States sell Pakistan $68 million worth of anti-aircraft missiles. He also promised that the United States would increase the aid for Pakistan's war on drugs by $1.5 million to $7.2 million.

In their private talks President Bush and Prime Minister Bhutto deviated from the positions of their two immediate predecessors. Now that the Soviet Union had withdrawn from Afghanistan, both leaders supported a political solution between the Soviet-backed regime in Kabul and the United States- and Pakistan-backed mujahedin rebels. They also discussed the attempts by Pakistan to develop nuclear weapons. United States intelligence reports had indicated that Pakistan was going forward in its development of nuclear weapons. However, Prime Minister Bhutto told President Bush and the press that she was a strong supporter of halting the proliferation of nuclear weapons. Also, she hoped that the United States would use its influence to prevent a nuclear arms race in South Asia. President Bush needed to certify to the Congress that Pakistan did not have nuclear weapons or the Congress would deny any further aid payments to Pakistan.

Prime Minister Bhutto addressed many of the same issues when she spoke to a joint session of Congress on June 7, 1989. Many in the audience were impressed by her speech, and some members of Congress said her speech was more eloquent than most of the ones they hear. Prime Minister Bhutto told the Congress about the advances for democracy that she symbolized. She said that, "Everywhere the sun is setting on the day of the dictator, the generals are returning to the barracks." She also reassured Congress that she did not want to be a party to a nuclear arms race in South Asia. Her speech went a long way toward insuring the continuation of aid to Pakistan.

At the 338th Harvard University Commencement on June 9, 1989, Prime Minister Benazir Bhutto received an honorary doctor of laws degree and gave the commencement address. She called for the democratic countries of the world to help countries such as Pakistan as they struggle to offer people basic human rights and a democratic government. Twenty-five thousand people stood in the rain to listen to this 1973 graduate of Harvard, impressed by her oratory and her message.

As Benazir Bhutto completes her first year in office and this book was being sent to the typesetter, the political situation in Pakistan remains unsettled. In the fall of 1989, Benazir Bhutto and her coalition government faced a serious challenge from opposition leaders. The opposition was able to collect enough votes to call for a no-confidence vote in the National Assembly. If Prime Minister Bhutto's government lost the no-confidence vote, then President Ishaq

Khan would be free to ask the opposition to form a new government. In the weeks preceding the vote, rumors circulated claiming that members of the National Assembly were offered as much as; one million dollars to switch sides. The rumors of vote-buying were substantiated by Assembly members on both sides. On November 4, 1989, Prime Minister Bhutto won the no-confidence vote by a slim eleven votes in the 236-seat Assembly.

It soon became apparent that Ms. Bhutto had made a few deals of her-own. Three opposition party members were given cabinet-level appointments within the Bhutto government in exchange for their support. It appears, at least for the time being, that Prime Minister Bhutto will continue in office and may now have quieted the opposition leaders enough to move forward.

The fact is that Benazir Bhutto and the Pakistan People's Party have had to spend much of their efforts trying to maintain their hold on the government. In many ways this has prevented Prime Minister Bhutto from enacting many of the reforms that she had promised in her election campaign. In some ways, conditions within Pakistan have changed little in a year. Illiteracy, poverty, corruption, and drug trafficking still continue as serious problems. Looked at in another light, the first year of Benazir Bhutto's leadership is remarkable. Freedom and democracy, which General Zia had wiped out, have returned.

The military, which has taken over the country four times in its brief history, has stayed out of politics. Even in the face of the disruption caused by the no-confidence vote, the generals have remained quiet. The problems that faced Benazir Bhutto seemed insurmountable when she was elected in December 1988. With the no-confidence vote behind her, there is renewed hope among many in Pakistan that this amazing woman can begin to solve some of those problems.

Her first year in office has shown her to be a competent diplomat who has garnered respect for herself and her country among the leaders of the rest of the world. She has been especially successful in getting the United States to renew its pledge of financial support to Pakistan.

On January 25, 1990 Benazir Bhutto achieved another first. She became the first leader of a modern state to give birth to a child while in office. The seven-pound, eight-ounce baby girl, whom they named Bakhtawar, is the second child of Ms. Bhutto and her husband, Asif Ali Zardari.

The First Benazir Bhutto Government (1988-1990)

On 2nd December 1988 Benazir Bhutto (BB), daughter of Zulfikar Ali Bhutto, who was executed in 1979 by the Zia-ul-Haq regime, was sworn in as Prime Minister of Pakistan. This was preceded by a convincing victory of her party, the PPP, despite manipulations on the part of the Pakistani establishment. The majority of Pakistani people, after more than a decade of military dictatorship, wanted a return of democratic conditions. Nevertheless, BB saw herself forced to make political concessions even before taking office. On the question of the appointment of the President, as well as foreign and security political matters, she had to a large extent, compromise and agree to the agenda of the military and conservative camps in the country.

Efforts by her government to increase their political maneuvering capabilities and decision areas soon led to a collision with the interests of the establishment. Twenty months after her accession to power, on 6th August 1990, President Ghulam Ishaq Khan (GIK) dismissed the BB government and dissolved the national parliament, as well as the parliaments of Sindh and NWFP in which the PPP had also formed the provincial governments. Apart from a fundamental dislike of the establishment against the Bhutto factor in Pakistan's politics and a substantial slandering campaign on the side of the Opposition and other circles, errors and failures in the government camp had also led to this development. Altogether, the first BB government had made no convincing impression on the majority of their friends and supporters. The obvious lack of experience and missing political visions had also contributed to their premature end.

Naturally many posed the question later whether BB and her first government had had any chance at all to remain for a full legislative period in office. Many answer this in the negative; however, it is always afterwards that everyone is smarter. It is certain that the President, like huge parts of the bureaucratic and feudal establishment, from the outset on worked to make life for the government difficult. Regarding the army, Commanding Officer of Army Staff Aslam Beg, who was neither a Punjabi nor Pathan but a Mohajir, was relatively open to the new government from the very beginning. Beg, a political general, tried to take on the role of an advisor, possibly with the hope of extending his term in office or for a political career later. BB felt Aslam Beg's advice efforts becoming increasingly patronizing. She therefore undertook steps to extend her own freedom away from the army which resulted in COAS Aslam Beg turning from her. Iqbak Akhund, National Security and Foreign Affairs Advisor in BB's first government, might have particularly dissuaded his boss regarding Beg's suggestion on the creation of a National Security Council. According to Beg's opinion, the absence of consultations between the basic political entities of the country within a top level committee was the cause for the past military coups in Pakistan's short history. Akhund, however, saw in such a committee the attempt of the military to control and influence the politicians and to force them to toe the line.

The appointment of Shamsur Rehman Kallue as DG ISI, which BB later admitted as an error, and the installation of a committee under Air Marshal (retd) Zulfikar Ali Khan for the investigation of the security agencies situation were steps which were disliked by the army and seen as interference in their own matters.

An open crisis between the military and government came in May 1990 when Beg ordered army units to crack down on the bloody uprising between the two main communities in the city of Hyderabad. Benazir Bhutto, not only Head of Government but also a Sindhi, feared a preferential treatment of MQM followers and a discrimination of the Sindhis and refused to issue a carte'-blanche' for further army operations in the troubled province of Sindh.

Some analysts were at the time and are even today, of the opinion that PM Benazir Bhutto should have taken the interference of the army in Hyderabad as the reason for her resignation. According to the Constitution she would have had to continue in office and therefore would have been able to create a good starting position for her in the new elections. By missing this strategic move, she paved the way for President Ghulam Ishaq Khan to dismiss her government a few months later and to appoint a caretaker government of his own choice. He had obtained the consent of the army well beforehand, in a meeting of the Corps Commanders on 21st July 1990 a dismissal of the BB government had been already agreed upon.

A Repetition of History (1993-1996)

The second BB government began in autumn 1993. With the elections on 6th and 8th October, the PPP emerged as the winner against the PML, led by Nawaz Sharif. Apart from that, BB succeeded a month later in bringing in Sardar Farooq Ahmed Khan *"one of her trustworthy associate for last many years"* to the Presidential Chair. For 30 years, Leghari had been a faithful and active PPP fighter. Therefore, at the end of 1993 the political horizon shone brightly for BB and her party. Very little indicated that scarcely three years later, there would be a repetition of her political fall in 1990. On 5th November 1996 the second BB government again came to a premature end. Like President Ghulam Ishaq Khan in the year 1990, Leghari also made accusations regarding mismanagement and corruption, thereby dismissing her government and dissolving the National Assembly.

Today, supporters of BB willingly comment on the second fall of the government with a reference to Karl Marx, whereby *"history always repeats itself, the first time as a tragedy, the* second time as a farce."

Analysing the cause for the second failure, reference must once again be made to the so-called Establishment—the syndicate comprising of the military, top bureaucrats, feudals, wealthy land owners and powerful businessmen. Though in the meantime names had changed in the top echelon of the military, the dislike against the PPP generally and, in particular, the Bhutto name in Pakistan's politics still existed. Many generals still felt indebted to Zia-ul-Haq for their careers. They had formed an oligarchy with him and had stood on Zia's side during the conviction case and the execution of Zulfikar Ali Bhutto.

Another reason for her downfall was that months earlier interested circles were successful in sowing distrust between the President and the Prime Minister. This distrust developed into political rivalry and personal enmity. The killing of Murtaza Bhutto on 20th September 1955 and the consequent accusation campaign against BB and her husband, Asif Ali Zardari, was part of a scheme aimed at ensuring the elimination of the Bhutto name from Pakistani politics.

However, there were without a doubt, also corruption scandals and mismanagement which had contributed to the fall of the second BB government. The majority of former PPP voters, who had seen the hand of the establishment behind the fall in 1990 and had still remained faithful, grew silent with the second downfall—disappointment and resignation reigned. BB herself also ascribed her defeat in the following elections in 1997 to the corruption charges against her, her husband and her government. She commented on this once by saying, *"some of which might be right and some wrong"*.

In addition, she correctly referred to it as the country's usual practice, saying *"...corruption is used as a pretext... to defame politicians and parliamentarians"*. She could have added that those who live in glass houses should not throw stones.

For the sake of fairness, here is once again her former fellow comrade and advisor, Iqbal Akhund, who in a summary over the achievements of both BB governments wrote: *"Her first* term was notable for its focus on human rights and, especially, the attention paid to the condition of women. The government took action against drug barons, against terrorism in the cities and banditry in the countryside; in her second term, the economy showed promise and foreign investors were beginning to discover Pakistan. An objective assessment of her performance does not leave one with an impression of exceptional wrong-doing and malfeasance".

The majority of her old stalwarts and former voters would today probably agree to this opinion again. In South Asia, people are willing to forgive and forget; therefore all is not completely lost for the PPP and their leader, Benazir Bhutto.

The Return of the Generals

When General Musharraf took over power in October 1999 by a coup d'état, BB was already, for months, in self-imposed political exile abroad and her husband, Asif Ali Zardari, was once again in detention. First hopes of the PPP leadership of coming to an agreement with the military could not be fulfilled. The main reason for the generals' seizure of power was their complete distrust in both previous political leaderships of the country, namely the governments of Nawaz Sharif and Benazir Bhutto. As the majority of the people at that time also carried strong reproaches against the politicians of the country, they welcomed General Musharraf.

Corruption and defraudation cases already initiated by the Nawaz Sharif government against BB, her husband Zardari and other PPP party members continued further. New cases were added on and in particular, Asif Ali Zardari was accused in the Murtaza Bhutto case. In the other camp, Nawaz Sharif had to watch how, only a few months after his overthrow, the majority of his former fellow followers and beneficiaries dropped him and offered themselves to the generals. The generals transformed the Muslim League into a new Kings party. Nawaz Sharif's attempts to stop this process through the tentative return of his family members to Lahore and thereby testing the possibility of his own return failed. The military reacted to this by promoting the Chaudhry's from Gujarat, who had always been political rivals of the Sharif's.

In the national elections on 10th October 2002, the remaining Nawaz Sharif faithfuls had to contest as PML-Nawaz (PML-N). They formed, by far, the smaller part of the previous Pakistan Muslim League. Flying under the banner of Mohammad Ali Jinnah, the majority contested as PML-QA and, being the King's party, achieved the most seats but had no majority. With the active assistance from the military camp, Chaudhry Shujaat Hussain and his fellow contestants finally formed the government. Mir Zafarullah Khan Jamali from Balochistan became their first Prime Minister.

The Splitting of the PPP

In the early stages after the take-over, Benazir Bhutto had more success in holding her party together. The PPP leaders initially resisted the offerings of the Musharraf camp. Only at the beginning of the third year of the military rule, the first cracks became visible. Aftab Ahmed Khan Sherpao, the former powerful and successful PPP Chief Minister in North-West-Frontier-Province (NWFP), returned in January 2002 from his exile in London. He had fled Pakistan two years earlier due to corruption charges filed against him. His return was based on an agreement with the new ruling powers, offering a new political chapter for him. The price he had to pay was the dropping of his party leader, Benazir Bhutto. In March 2002, Sherpao created his own party wing, PPP-Sherpao (PPP-S), in his home province NWFP and successfully contested in the national and province elections in October as an independent group.

If Sherpao was initially just one individual case, the clear break in the PPP came after the elections on 10th October 2002. In Islamabad on 14th November ten PPP representatives of the newly elected National Parliament announced the establishment of a forward bloc within the party. Their spokesmen were two long-standing and die-hard party cadres, Rao Sikandar Iqbal and Syed Faisal Saleh Hayat, who announced the intention of their group to vote for the PML-QA candidate, Jamali, as Prime Minister and to support him in the formation of his government. They argued that the deadlock caused by the election results had to be broken, paving the way for the transition from military to parliamentary rule.

Agreements between them and the military rulers were denied. However, on 23rd November six of these dissidents were promoted to Ministers in the new Jamali cabinet. Hayat and Sikandar became Ministers for Interior and Defence, respectively. A day later, on 24th November 2002 the Rubicon was finally crossed. The renegades created their own party wing, the PPPP, whereby the fourth P stood for Patriots. The electoral committee, as the highest national supervisory board, was informed and posed no objections - the PPP Patriots was born and the old PPP was hereby split.

Apart from the enticement of office and power, there were also strong internal party reasons for the defection of the so-called Patriots. Criticism and reproaches from them and also from remaining members of the PPP were directed towards the party leadership. BB was accused of lacking political flexibility, being egocentric and out of touch with reality. She was accused of concentrating too much on her and her husband's political rehabilitation, which included political freedom after returning to Pakistan.

Correctly, it must be also mentioned here that Faisal Saleh Hayat, who once had a special bond of trust with the young Benazir Bhutto, well before his defection had travelled to Dubai for discussions, in order to encourage BB to have a more flexible attitude in relation to the political conditions in Pakistan. He had no success; most likely the threat of splitting was even not discussed. However, due to this journey many PPP stalwarts today do not see him as an immediate traitor.

His critics and opponents however see him as a dissident, who sold himself to rescue his own skin. They refer to his release only two months before the elections, from many months of detention by the National Accountability Bureau, NAB. Even so, the corruption charges against him were not dismissed, thereby serving as a safety device against a possible political re-orientation.

Party Leadership by Remote Directive

For party president Benazir Bhutto, sitting in Dubai, only a few remedies remained to counteract against the deterioration of her party. By telephone, e-mail and meetings in Dubai and London with the most important cadres, she sought to hold the PPP together—the era of party leadership by remote directive had began.

PPP Vice President, Makhdoom Amin Fahim, who met General Musharraf on several occasions, turned out to be *"BB's most trusted lieutenant"*. He obeyed and implemented all her instructions regarding political statements, coalition strategies, nomination of candidates, etc., even when he was of another opinion. In doing so, he had to refuse all political advances offered to him by the military rulers. He also received criticism from several party cadres, regarding his soft stance against Benazir. Some others favored the return of Benazir Bhutto to Pakistan before the 2002 elections. They reasoned that a party Chairperson behind bars and participating in the elections would have been a beacon of light for the party's vote bank, resulting in a good election outcome.

Benazir Bhutto did not follow these recommendations, whether a flagging will for political struggle was the cause is not clear. She might have had in memory how hard the military dealt with Nawaz Sharif, in his more than one year of detention. In Dubai, she had to care for her ill mother and three growing children, whose father was imprisoned and who was more and more becoming a stranger to them. The decisive factor was, most likely, her thought to have more political maneuvering space in freedom than behind bars. Besides, she wouldn't have been allowed to contest the elections. On 2nd September 2002 the electoral committee had disqualified her because of her non-appearance before court in a so-called corruption case.

The possibilities of breaking open the political isolation seemed to emerge for the PPP after the 2002 elections, in which the party fared surprisingly well. Disappointed by the results of their King's Party and surprised by the success of the MMA, Musharraf & Co. initially seemed willing and ready to bring PPP and PML-Q together in the form of a coalition government. Makhdoom Amin Fahim had to reject this at the behest of BB.

Nevertheless, for him the door to the PM Office seemed to be open once more. Within the framework of the Alliance for Restoration of Democracy (ARD), he had negotiated with the remaining parliamentarians of PML-N and with the Islamic party alliance, MMA. Amin Fahim saw himself just short of the goal of becoming Prime Minister of such a coalition government. However BB, with whose consent Amin Fahim was talking with PML-N and MMA, called off the venture literally on the last day.

The reasons are unclear: she might have feared to sit together with the religious leaders in the same boat or was probably still hoping to come into business with the generals. The latter did not happen as BB had placed terms and conditions which were not acceptable for Musharraf. Her demands were the cancellation of all on-going proceedings against her and Zardari as well as her return in freedom and the possibility of a full political activity in the near future. In doing so, she overplayed her cards. The military soon dropped the idea of the political use of the PPP. Even in Sindh, the home province of the Bhuttos where the PPP achieved their greatest election results, the party was kept out of power.

As a further consequence, pressure from NAB was increasingly exercised on susceptible PPP cadres, causing some more defectors. PPP leaders who loudly and openly criticised the General and his followers landed up in prison. So was this the case of ex-Speaker Raza Yousuf Gilani, who was detained for long time after facing a dubious case in court.

Present day and Future Prospects

How does the situation look now at the end of the year 2005?

Aftab Khan Sherpao is today Minister for Interior and Faisal Saleh Hayat, who held that post for a long time, is currently Minister for Kashmir and Northern Areas. Rao Sikandar Iqbal is Senior Minister for Defence.

The house in Lahore rented by the PPP and called Bilawal House, which was to serve Asif Ali Zardari as headquarters for his project of revitalising the party and its supporters, has been deserted for months. Zardari is once again abroad, health problems have forced him to travel to London and New York. Evidently, he has to pay the price of eight years detention, which was obviously not such a luxury time as often publicized by his gaolers. Meanwhile, his exempt from detention on bail is recalled on dubious arguments; his return to Pakistan is therefore threatened with renewed arrest. The Zardari case remains a portrayal of the unholy alliance between politics and law in Pakistan today.

Furthermore, BB continues to fight corruption charges. Her opponents are trying to get a conviction on cases abroad which can then be propagandistic exploited on the home front. She currently faces charges in Switzerland and England. In addition and clearly recognisable is the on-going intention of the establishment to further split the PPP leadership and to weaken the party. Their goal is to form a new PPP, including all dissidents, which would emerge as a new strong secular party. The new party would be allotted the traditional PPP election symbol, trying therefore in this way to marginalise Benazir Bhutto and her followers.

On 9th February 2005, the Pakistan daily papers reported the merging of PPP- Patriots and PPP- Sherpao into a party which simply calls itself PPP. Rao Sikandar Iqbal commented on the merger as follows: *We have merged to serve our people on the political lines set by* Zulfikar Ali Bhutto and Hayat Mohammad Khan Sherpao 37 years ago."

There were occasional contacts between emissaries of the military and the top leadership of the PPP during the past two years; however no substantial change of the situation was seen. The belief in some PPP circles that Zardari's release in 2004 was the result of a more moderate attitude and understanding of the military towards the PPP, including BB, seems to be purely wishful thinking. A more realistic assessment of the situation was given by a political analyst of the party, who wrote in an internal party paper in August 2003, as follows:

> "The military president looks at the situation through the prism of his own malevolence: while he serially violates the substance of democracy, he can not do without its semblance. But for this, he appears to have any number of puppets willing—nay eager—to do his bidding and to sing and swing on the strings of his chosen puppeteers. The support of the PPP is to him no longer of any consequence, in his eyes, the Party is now dispensable. Indeed, a rare consensus has formed among the khakis of almost every stripe that the PPP has missed the bus, slipped the bonds of reason, spurned offers of conciliation, and embraced the path of blood and the way of confrontation.

BB is seen by them as one who time and again fails to distinguish the wood of reality from the trees of inconsequentiality and who has transcended the bounds of even her own party—triumph over a divided and doctrinally uncertain opposition, and raising up a circle of satraps beholden only to her as the supreme leader. In the military view, BB lacks the political acumen to understand that politics best functions in the realm of grey and not in the stark shades of black and white. It was shocking to see that these views of the khakis are shared by many members of the Party."

In a report on the Local Body Elections in 2005, the prestigious monthly magazine, Newsline, comments on the PPP results as follows, *"...the PPP's dismal performance in Sindh was also* a reflection of the growing internal conflict in the party's cadre."

Indeed, it is true that Benazir's party stands largely smoking under internal pressure, the cadre is split into two camps. One camp demands realpolitik and is ready to compromise with the present rulers. For them Bhuttoism has become its own political value, not necessarily connected to the presence of a Bhutto anymore. In other words, the PPP can also exist without being totally dependent on BB.

The other camp, led by Amin Fahim, sets further on an intransigent leadership of the party by BB. For them, not only is the charisma of the name Bhutto indispensable, they also agree with Benazir's uncompromising demands for the return to democratic conditions.

The internal divide within the PPP also make it impossible to come out with decisions of significance, for example, the resignation of all opposition members from all parliaments. In doing so, the semi-democratic character of the political setup in current Pakistan could be more clearly shown to the world public. But, as the PPP itself seem to be divided on such issues, they certainly cannot table and demand it from the ARD. Both camps within the PPP set their hopes now on the upcoming elections in 2007. However, as the local body elections 2005 have shown, there is not much reason for optimism.

The question is what can and what will BB further do? On the one hand, she must practice prudence in her utterances to incidents and developments in Pakistan. Islamabad, at present, is quick in attacking her on her so-called unpatriotic behavior. This was the case, for example, when BB mentioned doubts that Dr. A.Q. Khan had sold nuclear technology on his own initiative. Naturally, the military leadership felt accused and reacted sharply.

On the other hand, it was in BB's interest to remind the public that her father had made that historic decision regarding Pakistan's nuclear programme and that she, as PM, had handled the nuclear issue carefully.

An internal party paper from March 2004, which was approved by her, reports:

> "Shaheed Zulfikar Ai Bhutto was the architect of Pakistan's nuclear programme...Mohtamar Bhutto protected the nuclear programme given by Shaheed Bhutto from international onslaught through the 'Benazir Nuclear Doctrine'... The recent nuclear export scandal poses great dangers to Pakistan's core interests of sovereignty, integrity and nuclear assets.
>
> The Government has handled the issue most thoughtlessly. By making a scapegoat of the scientists it has given an opportunity to the international community to file an FIR against us, which can be open any time. It has confessed that its command and control structure as well as its armed forces security and intelligence gathering was too weak to prevent a handful of scientists from proliferating all the way from Timbucktoo to Malaysia…The PPP has all along maintained that the scientists are being scapegoated to cover up the faults of others."

After the assassination of her brother Murtaza, she gave an interview in the Time Magazine. On the question on whether she would strive once more for the PM office, her answer was as follows:

> "No, I don't. Why should I?... for me, the prime ministership means hard work. My father worked from morning to night. I worked from morning to night. What did my father get? He got hanged. What did I get? I got slandered..."

However, this interview had taken place before her second downfall, a removal from office which was accompanied by a massive smear campaign against her and the name Bhutto. She knows that the execution of her father has left a scar on the soul of the nation and she will feel obligated to return honor and recognition to the Bhutto name. She will therefore not give up her fight against an establishment which hung her father, hunted her from her office, murdered, in her view, her two brothers and defiled the family name. She will feel obliged to continue her fight for the reputation of the Bhutto Dynasty. She might see this also as her duty to her growing children. Last but not least she will feel committed to the Pakistani people as many of them still have a lot of trust in the Bhutto name.

The fact that the country presently stands once again under military rule will give her the incentive. She will try to get assistance from outside in particular from the West. Her political experience tells her that the present honeymoon between Washington and Islamabad cannot last forever. She will rely on the fact that in the post—Bush period, Washington will again strengthen her demands on human rights and democratic standards—therefore her fight cannot be seen as hopeless and futile.

12

The Murder

Daughter of the East Benazir Bhutto was assassinated on Thursday. The two-time Pakistan Prime Minister had finished addressing an election meeting in the garrison town of Rawalpindi and was leaving the venue in her car when the assailant struck.

As Benazir's white four-wheel drive waded through crowds of party supporters, she waved to the crowds through a rolled down window. This was when five shots rang out. The bullets pierced through the windshield, two of them caught her in the chest and neck and she slumped in her seat.

The killer tried to escape, but when he found himself trapped in the crowd of supporters, he blew himself up killing more than 30 and injuring scores of others. It all happened in a matter of minutes. Camera footage showed Benazir cheerful in a purple and white salwar suit waving at her supporters. Her cavalcade had barely pulled out when the bullets got her.

As chaos and utter confusion prevailed, her supporters rushed her to the General Hospital in Rawalpindi, where she was declared dead at 6.16 pm, Pakistan time.

"Before she was brought to the hospital, her heart had

stopped beating and her breathing had stopped. Immediate efforts were made to revive her and restore her breathing but unfortunately we couldn't succeed," a doctor who attended on her confirmed. It is possible that the impact of the blast had caused her heart to stop.

As soon as news of her death broke, Bhutto's suporters exploded in anger, smashing the glass door at the main entrance of the emergency unit of the hospital. Others burst into tears. One man with a Pakistan People's Party flag tied around his head beat his chest in sorrow. "Killer, killer Musharraf" slogans went up against the Pakistan President.

Violent Pakistan People's Party (PPP) supporters raced through Karachi, Benazir's home town, and angry partymen wrecked whatever came their way. Reports of large-scale violence came in from Karachi, Rawalpindi and Peshawar.

House after the assassination, President Pervez Musharraf appealed for calm and said he was shocked. He summoned an emergency meeting at the Presidency. Addressing the nation on national television, a grim Musharraf conveyed his condolences to the family of Benazir Bhutto and those who died in the blast. He declared a three-day national mourning. "The national flag will be at half mast as a mark of respect to the departed leader," he said. He reiterated his resolve to crush terrorism with a heavy hand.

Nawaz Sharif, another former Prime Minister of Pakistan, Pakistan Muslim League leader and a key player in the January 8 polls, reached the hospital hours later. He was campaigning some distance away and rushed when he got to know of Benazir's assassination. He looked shaken and barely spoke as he sat silently beside Bhutto's body. He later told reporters he'd take forward Bhutto's fight.

As doctors made frantic efforts to revive Benazir, the government initially issued a statement claiming she was in no danger. But her senior party leaders quickly contacted the media and rebutted the statement. In fact, the confirmation of her being in real and present danger came from her husband, Asif Ali Zardari, who lives in Dubai with their three children.

He told a private TV channel about her critical condition and asked the Pakistani people to pray for her life. Minutes later, a party official confirmed she was no more.

Bhutto was in Rawalpindi as part of her election campaign. She was addressing an election rally at the same park where former Pakistan Prime Minister Liaquat Ali Khan had been assassinated in 1951.

Bhutto's party leaders hit out at the government for not heeding their requests for tighter security for Bhutto. Only a day before, on Wednesday, a young man was arrested with explosives close to the venue of her public meeting in Peshawar.

Within hours of the assassination, condemnations poured in from Washington, Moscow and London. Prime Minister Manmohan Singh reacted with shock and horror, A US spokesperson described the killing as an attempt to disrupt Pakistan's efforts to rebuild democracy

Thursday's murderous attack was the second major attempt on Bhutto's life in less than three months. A march she was heading in Karachi was attacked on the intervening night of October 18 and October 19 after she landed in her country after spending almost eight years in exile. More than 150 of her party workers were killed in that suicide blast. Bhutto remained unscathed though her vehicle was badly damaged and some of her senior party leaders badly injured.

Bhutto had later blamed the attack on three people in the Pervez Musharraf government. She had studiously avoided going public with their names, but said she had written to Musharraf before her arrival in the country about the danger to her life.

But unlike her, senior leaders in her party hadn't minced words. They had named erstwhile chief minister of Punjab Chaudhry Fervaiz Elahi, then federal religious minister Ejazul

Haq and the Intelligence Bureau chief, Brigadier (retired) Ejaz Shah, as the three people involved in hatching the plot. Bhutto never denied her supporters' claims.

All three are closely associated with President Musharraf and at least two have some personal reasons to oppose her which go back decades.

Elahi is the son-in-law of Chaudhary Eahoor Elahi, a leader of the Pakistan Muslim League who was among the main opposition leaders during plan the government of Zulfikar Ali Bhutto between 1911-1977.

He was later killed in an attack in Lahore in September 1981. His family accused Al-Zulfikar, an organisation allegedly run by Bhutto's brother Mir Murtaza, for the killing.

Haq is the son of General Zia-ul-Haq who overthrew the Zulfikar Ali Bhutto government in 1977 and later hanged him after what is euphemistically called a mis-trial in Pakistan's judicial history.

Shah, the last man in the trio, is widely believed to be a personal friend of President Musharraf from their military days and worked as home secretary in Punjab before taking over as the head of one of the two major intelligence agencies.

The government, however, has consistently denied the complicity of these people in any plan to assassinate Bhutto. The authorities have time and again warned that she was a major target for Islamic militants for her opposition to their brand of conservative Islam.

Though no militant group has taken responsibility for issuing any threats against her, she has always faced sustained criticism and vociferous opposition from religious circles, especially the fundamentalist radicals, for her unorthodox religious views.

Bhutto, too, had at one point of time alleged that Osama Bin Laden had been working against her. In fact, she had accused him of plotting the overthrow of her government in the 1990s through attempts to bribe legislators to vote against her in a no-confidence move.

13

Overview

Benazir Bhutto was born in Karachi, Dominion of Pakistan on 21 June 1953. She attended the Lady Jennings Nursery School and then the Convent of Jesus and Mary in Karachi. After two years of schooling at the Rawalpindi Presentation Convent, she was sent to the Jesus and Mary Convent at Murree. She passed her O-level examination at the age of 15. She then went on to complete her A-Levels at the Karachi Grammar School.

After completing her early education in Pakistan, she pursued her higher education in the United States. From 1969 to 1973 she attended Radcliffe College, and then Harvard University, where she obtained a Bachelor of Arts degree with cum laude honors in comparative government. She was also elected to Phi Beta Kappa.

The next phase of her education took place in the United Kingdom. Between 1973 and 1977 Bhutto studied Philosophy, Politics, and Economics at Lady Margaret Hall, Oxford. She completed a course in International Law and Diplomacy while at Oxford. In December 1976 she was elected president of the Oxford Union, becoming the first Asian woman to head the prestigious debating society.

On 18 December 1987 she married Asif Ali Zardari in

Karachi. The couple had three children: Bilawal, Bakhtwar, and Aseefa.

Family

Benazir Bhutto's father, former Prime Minister Zulfikar Ali Bhutto, was dismissed as Prime Minister in 1975, on charges similar to those Benazir Bhutto would later face. Later, in a 1977 trial on charges of conspiracy to murder the father of dissident politician Ahmed Raza Kasuri, Zulfikar Ali Bhutto was sentenced to death.

Despite the accusation being "widely doubted by the public", and despite many clemency appeals from foreign leaders, Zulfikar Ali Bhutto was hanged on 4 April 1979. Appeals for clemency were dismissed by acting President General Muhammad Zia-ul-Haq. Benazir Bhutto and her mother were held in a "police camp" until the end of May, after the execution.

In 1985, Benazir Bhutto's brother Shahnawaz was killed under suspicious circumstances, in France. The killing of another of her brothers, Mir Murtaza, in 1996, contributed to destabilizing her second term as Prime Minister.

Prime Minister

Bhutto, who had returned to Pakistan after completing her studies, found herself placed under house arrest in the wake of her father's imprisonment and subsequent execution. Having been allowed in 1984 to return to the United Kingdom, she became a leader in exile of the Pakistan Peoples Party (PPP), her father's party, though she was unable to make her political presence felt in Pakistan until after the death of General Muhammad Zia-ul-Haq. She had succeeded her mother as leader of the Pakistan People's Party and the pro-democracy opposition to the Zia-ul-Haq regime.

On 16 November 1988, in the first open election in more than a decade, Bhutto's PPP won the largest bloc of seats in the National Assembly. Bhutto was sworn in as Prime Minister of a coalition government on 2 December, becoming at age 35 the youngest person—and the first woman—to head the government of a Muslim-majority state in modern times. That same year, People Magazine included Ms. Bhutto in its list of The Fifty Most Beautiful People. In 1989, she was awarded the Prize For Freedom by the Liberal International.

Bhutto's government was dismissed in 1990 following charges of corruption, for which she never was tried. Zia's protégé Nawaz Sharif subsequently came to power. Bhutto was re-elected in 1993 but was dismissed three years later amid various corruption scandals by then president Farooq Leghari, who used the Eighth Amendment discretionary powers to dissolve the government. The Supreme Court affirmed President Leghari's dismissal in a 6-1 ruling. In 2006, Interpol issued a request for arrest of Bhutto and her husband.

The criticism against Bhutto came largely from the Punjabi elites and powerful landlord families who opposed Bhutto as she pushed Pakistan into nationalist reform, opposing feudals, whom she blamed for the destabilization of Pakistan.

Musharraf's disqualification

On 17 September 2007 Benazir Bhutto accused Pervez Musharraf's allies of pushing Pakistan into crisis by their refusal to permit democratic reforms and power-sharing. A nine-member panel of Supreme Court judges deliberated on six petitions (including one from Jamaat-e-Islami, Pakistan's largest Islamic group) asserting that Musharraf be disqualified from contending for the presidency of Pakistan. Bhutto stated that her party could join one of the opposition groups, potentially that of Nawaz Sharif. Attorney-general Malik Mohammed Qayyum stated that, pendente lite, the Election Commission was "reluctant" to announce the schedule for the presidential vote. Bhutto's party's Farhatullah Babar stated that the Constitution could bar Musharraf from being elected again because he was already chief of the army: "As Gen. Musharraf was disqualified from contesting for President, he has prevailed upon the Election Commission to arbitrarily and illegally tamper with the Constitution of Pakistan."

Policies for Women

During election campaigns the Bhutto government voiced its concern for women's social and health issues, including the issue of discrimination against women. Bhutto announced plans to establish women's police stations, courts, and women's development banks. Despite these promises, Bhutto did not propose any legislation to improve welfare services for women. During her election campaigns, Bhutto promised to repeal controversial laws (such as Hudood and Zina ordinances) that curtail the rights of women in Pakistan. Her party never did fulfil these promises during her tenures as Prime Minister, due to immense pressure from the opposition.

Only after her stints as Prime Minister did her party initiate legislation to repeal the Zina ordinance, during General Musharraf's regime. These efforts were defeated by the right-wing religious parties that dominated the legislatures at the time.

Policy on Taliban

The Taliban took power in Kabul in September 1996. It was during Bhutto's rule that the Taliban gained prominence in Afghanistan. She viewed the Taliban as a group that could stabilize Afghanistan and enable trade access to the Central Asian republics, according to author Stephen Coll.[18] He claims that her government provided military and financial support for the Taliban, even sending a small unit of the Pakistani army into Afghanistan.

More recently, she took an anti-Taliban stance, and condemned terrorist acts committed by the Taliban and their supporters.

Exile

After being dismissed by the then-president of Pakistan on charges of corruption, her party lost the October elections. She served as leader of the opposition while Nawaz Sharif became Prime Minister for the next three years. Elections were held again in October 1993 and her PPP coalition was victorious, returning Bhutto to office. In 1996 her government was once again dismissed on corruption charges.

Charges of Corruption

French, Polish, Spanish, and Swiss documents have fueled the charges of corruption against Bhutto and her husband. Bhutto and her husband faced a number of legal proceedings, including a charge of laundering money through Swiss banks. Her husband, Asif Ali Zardari, spent eight years in prison on similar corruption charges. Zardari, released from jail in 2004, has suggested that his time in prison involved torture; human rights groups have supported his claim that his rights were violated.

A 1998 New York Times investigative report indicates that Pakistani investigators have documents that uncover a network of bank accounts, all linked to the family's lawyer in Switzerland, with Asif Zardari as the principal shareholder. According to the article, documents released by the French authorities indicated that Zardari offered exclusive rights to Dassault, a French aircraft manufacturer, to replace the air force's fighter jets in exchange for a 5% commission to be paid to a Swiss corporation controlled by Zardari. The article also said a Dubai company received an exclusive license to import gold into Pakistan for which Asif Zardari received payments of more than $10M into his Dubai-based Citibank accounts. The owner of the company denied that he had made payments to Zardari and claims the documents were forged.

Bhutto maintained that the charges leveled against her and her husband were purely political. "Most of those documents are fabricated," she said, "and the stories that have been spun around them are absolutely wrong." An Auditor General of Pakistan (AGP) report supports Bhutto's claim. It presents information suggesting that Benazir Bhutto was ousted from power in 1990 as a result of a witch hunt approved by then-president Ghulam Ishaq Khan. The AGP report says Khan illegally paid legal advisers 28 million Rupees to file 19 corruption cases against Bhutto and her husband in 1990-92.

The assets held by Bhutto and her husband have been scrutinized. The prosecutors have alleged that their Swiss bank accounts contain £740 million. Zardari also bought a neo-Tudor mansion and estate worth over £4 million in Surrey, England, UK. The Pakistani investigations have tied other overseas properties to Zardari's family. These include a $2.5 million manor in Normandy owned by Zardari's parents, who had modest assets at the time of his marriage. Bhutto denied holding substantive overseas assets.

Bhutto and her husband until recently continued to face wide-ranging charges of official corruption in connection with hundreds of millions of dollars of "commissions" on government contracts and tenders. But because of a power-sharing deal brokered in October 2007 between Bhutto and Musharraf, she and her husband had been granted amnesty. If it stood, this development could have triggered a number of Swiss banks to "unlock" accounts that were frozen in the late 1990s. The executive order could in principle have been challenged by the judiciary, although the judiciary's future was uncertain due to the same developments. However, the death of Bhutto has now prevented any such accounts from being unlocked, and it is now up to the discretion of the Swiss banks as to where the funds ought to be placed.

Switzerland

On 23 July 1998, the Swiss Government handed over documents to the government of Pakistan which relate to corruption allegations against Benazir Bhutto and her husband. The documents included a formal charge of money laundering by Swiss authorities against Zardari. The Pakistani government had been conducting a wide-ranging inquiry to account for more than $13.7 million frozen by Swiss authorities in 1997 that was allegedly stashed in banks by Bhutto and her husband. The Pakistani government recently filed criminal charges against Bhutto in an effort to track down an estimated $1.5 billion she and her husband are alleged to have received in a variety of criminal enterprises. The documents suggest that the money Zardari was alleged to have laundered was accessible to Benazir Bhutto and had been used to buy a diamond necklace for over $175,000.

The PPP has responded by flatly denying the charges, suggesting that Swiss authorities have been misled by false evidence provided by Islamabad.

On 6 August 2003, Swiss magistrates found Bhutto and her husband guilty of money laundering. They were given six-month suspended jail terms, fined $50,000 each and were ordered to pay $11 million to the Pakistani government. The six-year trial concluded that Bhutto and Zardari deposited in Swiss accounts $10 million given to them by a Swiss company in exchange for a contract in Pakistan. The couple said they would appeal. The Pakistani investigators say Zardari opened a Citibank account in Geneva in 1995 through which they say he passed some $40 million of the $100 million he received in payoffs from foreign companies doing business in Pakistan.

In October 2007, Daniel Zappelli, chief prosecutor of the canton of Geneva, said he received the conclusions of a money laundering investigation against former Pakistani Prime Minister Benazir Bhutto on Monday, October 29, but it was unclear whether there would be any further legal action against her in Switzerland.

Poland

The Polish Government has given Pakistan 500 pages of documentation relating to corruption allegations against

Benazir Bhutto and her husband. These charges are in regard to the purchase of 8,000 tractors in a 1997 deal. According to Pakistani officials, the Polish papers contain details of illegal commissions paid by the tractor company in return for agreeing to their contract. It was alleged that the arrangement "skimmed" Rs 103 mn rupees ($2 million) in kickbacks. "The documentary evidence received from Poland confirms the scheme of kickbacks laid out by Asif Ali Zardari and Benazir Bhutto in the name of (the) launching of Awami tractor scheme," APP said. Bhutto and Asif Ali Zardari allegedly received a 7.15% commission on the purchase through their front men, Jens Schlegelmilch and Didier Plantin of Dargal S.A., who received about $1.969 million for supplying 5,900 Ursus tractors.

France

Potentially the most lucrative deal alleged in the documents involved the effort by Dassault Aviation, a French military contractor. French authorities indicated in 1998 that Bhutto's husband, Zardari, offered exclusive rights to Dassault to replace the air force's fighter jets in exchange for a five percent commission to be paid to a corporation in Switzerland controlled by Zardari.

At the time, French corruption laws forbade bribery of French officials but permitted payoffs to foreign officials, and even made the payoffs tax-deductible in France. However, France changed this law in 2000.

Western Asia

In the largest single payment investigators have discovered, a gold bullion dealer in the Western Asia was alleged to have deposited at least $10 million into one of Zardari's accounts after the Bhutto government gave him a monopoly on gold imports that sustained Pakistan's jewellery industry. The money was allegedly deposited into Zardari's Citibank account in Dubai.

Pakistan's Arabian Sea coast, stretching from Karachi

to the border with Iran, has long been a gold smugglers' haven. Until the beginning of Bhutto's second term, the trade, running into hundreds of millions of dollars a year, was unregulated, with slivers of gold called biscuits, and larger weights in bullion, carried on planes and boats that travel between the Persian Gulf and the largely unguarded Pakistani coast.

Shortly after Bhutto returned as prime minister in 1993, a Pakistani bullion trader in Dubai, Abdul Razzak Yaqub, proposed a deal: in return for the exclusive right to import gold, Razzak would help the government regularize the trade. In November 1994, Pakistan's Commerce Ministry wrote to Razzak informing him that he had been granted a license that made him, for at least the next two years, Pakistan's sole authorized gold importer. In an interview in his office in Dubai, Razzak acknowledged that he had used the license to import more than $500 million in gold into Pakistan, and that he had travelled to Islamabad several times to meet with Bhutto and Zardari. But he denied that there had been any corruption or secret deals. "I have not paid a single cent to Zardari," he said.

Razzak claims that someone in Pakistan who wished to destroy his reputation had contrived to have his company wrongly identified as the depositor. "Somebody in the bank has cooperated with my enemies to make false documents," he said.

During Exile

2002 Election

The Bhutto-led Pakistan Peoples Party (PPP) secured the highest number of votes (28.42%) and eighty seats (23.16%) in the national assembly in the October 2002 general elections. Pakistan Muslim League (N) (PML-N) managed to win eighteen seats only. Some of the elected candidates of Pakistan Peoples Party formed a faction of their own, calling it PPP-Patriots which was being led by Makhdoom Faisal Saleh Hayat, the former leader of Bhutto-led PPP.

They later formed a coalition government with Musharraf's party, PML-Q.

Early 2000s

In 2002, Pakistani president Pervez Musharraf amended Pakistan's constitution to ban prime ministers from serving more than two terms. This disqualifies Bhutto from ever holding the office again. This move was widely considered to be a direct attack on former prime ministers Benazir Bhutto and Nawaz Sharif. On 3 August 2003, Bhutto became a member of Minhaj ul Quran International (An international Muslim educational and welfare organization).

From September 2004, Bhutto lived in Dubai, United Arab Emirates, where she cared for her children and her mother, who was suffering from Alzheimer's disease, travelling to give lectures and keeping in touch with the Pakistan Peoples Party's supporters. She and her three children were reunited with her husband and their father in December 2004 after more than five years.

On 27 January 2007 she was invited by the United States to speak to President Bush and congressional and State Department officials.

Bhutto appeared as a panellist on the BBC TV programme Question Time in the UK in March 2007. She has also appeared on BBC current affairs programme Newsnight on several occasions. She rebuffed comments made by Muhammad Ijaz-ul-Haq in May 2007 regarding the knighthood of Salman Rushdie, citing that he was calling for the assassination of foreign citizens.

Bhutto had declared her intention to return to Pakistan within 2007, which she did, in spite of Musharraf's statements of May 2007 about not allowing her to return ahead of the country's general election, due late 2007 or early 2008. It was speculated that she may have been offered the office of Prime Minister again.

Arthur Herman, a U.S. historian, in a controversial letter

published in The Wall Street Journal on 14 June 2007, in response to an article by Bhutto highly critical of the president and his policies, has described her as "One of the most incompetent leaders in the history of South Asia", and asserted that she and other elites in Pakistan hate Musharraf because he was a muhajir, the son of one of millions of Indian Muslims who fled to Pakistan during partition in 1947. Herman has claimed, "Although it was muhajirs who agitated for the creation of Pakistan in the first place, many native Pakistanis view them with contempt and treat them as third-class citizens."

Nonetheless, as of mid-2007, the US appeared to be pushing for a deal in which Musharraf would remain as president but step down as military head, and either Bhutto or one of her nominees would become prime minister.

On 11 July 2007, the Associated Press, in an article about the possible aftermath of the Red Mosque incident, wrote:

> Benazir Bhutto, the former prime minister and opposition leader expected by many to return from exile and join Musharraf in a power-sharing deal after year-end general elections, praised him for taking a tough line on the Red Mosque. I'm glad there was no cease-fire with the militants in the mosque because cease-fires simply embolden the militants," she told Britain's Sky TV on Tuesday. "There will be a backlash, but at some time we have to stop appeasing the militants."

This remark about the Red Mosque was seen with dismay in Pakistan as reportedly hundreds of young students were burned to death and remains are untraceable and cases are being heard in Pakistani supreme court as a missing persons issue. This and subsequent support for Musharaf led Elder Bhutto's comrades like Khar to criticize her publicly.

Bhutto however advised Musharraf in an early phase of the latter's quarrel with the Chief Justice, to restore him. Her PPP did not capitalize on its CEC member, Aitzaz, the chief Barrister for the Chief Justice, in successful restoration. Rather he was seen as a rival and was isolated.

Possible Deal with the Musharraf Government

This Section may Require Cleanup to Meet Wikipedia's Quality Standards

Please improve this article if you can (October 2007).

Talks between Musharraf and Bhutto in 2004 likely resulted in her husband's release.

In July 2007, some of Bhutto's frozen funds were released. Bhutto still faces significant charges of corruption. In an 8 August 2007 interview with the Canadian Broadcasting Corporation, Bhutto revealed the meeting focused on her desire to return to Pakistan for the 2008 elections, and of Musharraf retaining the Presidency with Bhutto as Prime Minister. On 29 August 2007, Bhutto announced that Musharraf would step down as chief of the army. On 1 September Bhutto vowed to return to Pakistan "very soon", regardless of whether or not she reached a power-sharing deal with Musharraf before then.

Many observers consider such a deal improbable. In summer 2002 Musharraf implemented a two-term limit on Prime Ministers. Both Bhutto and Musharraf's other chief rival, Nawaz Sharif, have already served two terms as Prime Minister. Musharraf's allies in parliament, especially the PMLQ, are unlikely to reverse the changes to allow Prime Ministers to seek third terms, nor to make particular exceptions for either Bhutto or Sharif.

On 17 September 2007, Bhutto accused Musharraf's allies of pushing Pakistan into crisis by their refusal to permit democratic reforms and power-sharing. A nine-member panel of Supreme Court judges deliberated on six petitions (including one from Jamaat-e-Islami, Pakistan's largest Islamic group) asserting that Musharraf be disqualified from contending for the presidency of Pakistan. Bhutto stated that her party could join one of the opposition groups, potentially that of Nawaz Sharif. Attorney-general Malik Mohammed Qayyum stated that, pendente lite, the Election Commission was "reluctant" to announce the schedule for the presidential vote. Bhutto's party's Farhatullah Babar stated that the Constitution could bar Musharraf from being elected again because he was already chief of the army: "As Gen. Musharraf was disqualified from contesting for President, he has prevailed upon the Election Commission to arbitrarily and illegally tamper with the Constitution of Pakistan."

On 2 October 2007, Gen. Musharraf named Lt. Gen. Ashfaq Kayani, as vice chief of the army starting 8 October with the intent that if Musharraf won the presidency and resigned his military post, Kayani would become chief of the army. Meanwhile, Minister Sheikh Rashid Ahmed stated that officials agreed to grant Benazir Bhutto amnesty versus pending corruption charges. She has emphasized the smooth transition and return to civilian rule and has asked Pervez Musharaf to shed uniform.

On 5 October 2007, Musharraf signed the National Reconciliation Ordinance, giving amnesty to Bhutto and other political leaders—except exiled former premier Nawaz Sharif—in all court cases against them, including all corruption charges. The Ordinance came a day before Musharraf faced the crucial presidential poll. Both Bhutto's oppsition party, the PPP, and the ruling PMLQ, were involved in negotiations beforehand about the deal. In return, Bhutto and the PPP agreed not to boycott the Presidential election.

On 6 October 2007, Musharraf won a parliamentary election for President. However, the Supreme Court ruled that no winner can be officially proclaimed until it finishes deciding on whether it was legal for Musharraf to run for President while remaining Army General. Bhutto's PPP party did not join the other opposition parties' boycott of the election, but did abstain from voting. Later, Bhutto demanded security coverage on-par with the President's. Bhutto also contracted foreign security firms for her protection.

Return to Pakistan and Assassination Attempts

After eight years in exile in Dubai and London, Bhutto returned to Karachi on 18 October 2007 to prepare for the 2008 national elections.

En route to a rally in Karachi on 18 October 2007, two explosions occurred shortly after Bhutto had landed and left Jinnah International Airport. She was not injured but the explosions, later found to be a suicide-bomb attack, killed 136 people and injured at least 450. The dead included at least 50 of the security guards from her Pakistan Peoples Party who had formed a human chain around her truck to keep potential bombers away, as well as 6 police officers. A number of senior officials were injured. Bhutto was escorted unharmed from the scene.

Bhutto later claimed that she had warned the Pakistani government that suicide bomb squads would target her upon her return to Pakistan and that the government had failed to act. She was careful not to blame Pervez Musharraf for the attacks, accusing instead "certain individuals [within the government] who abuse their positions, who abuse their powers" to advance the cause of Islamic militants. Shortly after the attempt on her life, Bhutto wrote a letter Musharraf naming four persons whom she suspected of carrying out the attack. Those named included Chaudhry Pervaiz Elahi, a rival PML-Q politician and chief minister of Pakistan's Punjab province, Hamid Gul, former director of the Inter-Services Intelligence, and Ijaz Shah, the director general of the Intelligence Bureau, another of the country's intelligence agencies. All those named are close associates of General Musharraf. Bhutto has a long history of accusing parts of the government, particularly Pakistan's premier military intelligence agencies, of working against her and her party because they oppose her liberal, secular agenda. Bhutto claimed that the ISI has for decades backed militant Islamic groups in Kashmir and in Afghanistan.

There are discrepancies between the accounts published in western newspapers, Pakistani tabloids, and eye witness accounts of the assassination attempt. Bhutto's husband categorically refused to accept that the suicide bombing was an attack by Al Qaeda or the Taliban. Correspondingly, Pakistani Taliban leader Mehsud denied responsibility and Jamaat Islami, an opponent of Bhutto, announced a three days mourning period for the dead, thus lending credibility to Bhutto's claims that the attack was engineered by close associates in the government of General Musharraf.

Bhutto's associates describe an initial small grenade attack, followed twenty seconds later by larger explosives, one right and and one left of the truck carrying Bhutto; this was followed by a brief burst of gun fire directed at vehicle's roof. The PPP sources claim that yet another non-exploded bomb was fixed on a bridge which the vehicle had already crossed.

Some witnesses report there was a sizzling sound, apparently an underground wire signal for the explosive devices. Bhutto escaped, as she was protected by a 30-inch (760 mm) tall bullet-proof lining on the top of the truck and was reportedly descending into the vehicle's interior at the time; hence neither shrapnel nor bullets killed her. She was also protected by a "human cordon" of supporters who had anticipated suicide attacks and formed a chain around her to prevent potential bombers from getting near her. The total number of injured, according to PPP sources, stood at 1000, with at least 160 dead (The New York Times claims 134 dead and about 450 injured). The PPP lodged a complaint and FIR in protest, but was cautious in laying blame.

A few days later, Bhutto's lawyer Senator Farooq H. Naik said he received a letter threatening to kill his client. The letter also claims to have links with al-Qaeda and followers of Osama bin Laden.

Bhutto was well aware of the risk to her own life that might result from here return from exile to campaign for the leadership position. In an interview on September 28, 2007, with reporter Wolf Blitzer of CNN, she readily admitted the possibility of attack on herself:

> WOLF BLITZER: . . . Michael Scheuer is a former CIA analyst, he ran the bin Laden unit at the CIA. We spoke with him earlier today. He said you've been targeted in the past, including by Ramzi Yousef, who was the mastermind of the 1993 World Trade Center bombing, and you will be targeted again. I just want to get back to this point. You got be very worried. What kind of security will you have when you go back there?
>
> BHUTTO: Well, I have raised the issue of my security with General Musharraf, and I've asked him to provide me the security that I'm entitled to as a former prime minister. I hope that he will provide me the security, because I have been a target of terrorists in the past. And I know I could be a target in the future.

Response to 2007 State of Emergency

Main article: *2007 Pakistani state of emergency*

On 3 November 2007, President Pervez Musharraf declared a state of emergency, citing actions by the Supreme Court of Pakistan and religious extremism in the nation. Bhutto returned to the country, interrupting a visit to family in Dubai. She was greeted by supporters chanting slogans at the airport. After staying in her plane for several hours she was driven to her home in Lahore, accompanied by hundreds of supporters. While acknowledging that Pakistan faced a political crisis, she noted that Musharraf's declaration of emergency, unless lifted, would make it very difficult to have fair elections. She commented that "The extremists need a dictatorship, and dictatorship needs extremists."

House Arrest

Wikinews has related news:

Pakistan Lifts House Arrest of Former PM Benazir Bhutto

On 8 November 2007, Bhutto was placed under house arrest just a few hours before she was due to lead and address a rally against the state of emergency. She made some attempts to come out of house arrest but police stopped her. All roads to her house were closed. The following day, the Pakistani government announced that Bhutto's arrest warrant had been withdrawn and that she would be free to travel and to appear at public rallies. However, leaders of other opposition political parties remained prohibited from speaking in public.

Preparation for 2008 Elections

On 24 November 2007, Bhutto filed her nomination papers for January's Parliamentary elections; two days later, she filed papers in the Larkana constituency for two regular seats. She did so as former Pakistani Prime Minster Nawaz Sharif, following seven years of exile in Saudi Arabia, made his much-contested return to Pakistan and bid for candidacy.

When sworn in again on 30 November 2007, this time as a civilian president after relinquishing his post as military chief, Musharraf announced his plan to lift the Pakistan's state of emergency rule on 16 December. Bhutto welcomed the announcement and launched a manifesto outlining her party's domestic issues. Bhutto told journalists in Islamabad that her party, the Pakistan People's Party, would focus on "the five E's": employment, education, energy, environment, equality.

On 4 December 2007, Bhutto met with Nawaz Sharif to publicize their demand that Musharraf fulfill his promise to lift the state of emergency before January's parliamentary elections, threatening to boycott the vote if he failed to comply. They promised to assemble a committee which would present to Musharraf the list of demands upon which their participation in the election was contingent.

On 8 December 2007 it was reported that three unidentified gunmen stormed Mrs. Bhutto's Pakistan

People's Party office in the southern western province of Baluchistan. It was confirmed by local police that three of Bhutto's supporters were killed.

Assassination

Main article: *Benazir Bhutto Assassination*

Wikinews has related news:

Benazir Bhutto killed in suicide attack

On 27 December 2007, Bhutto was killed while entering a vehicle upon leaving a political rally for the Pakistan People's Party in Rawalpindi, Pakistan. A suicidal assassin reportedly fired shots in Bhutto's direction just prior to detonating an explosive pellet-laden vest, killing approximately 22 people and wounding many more.

The attack occurred just after Bhutto left the rally, where she had given a campaign address to party supporters in the run-up to the January 2008 parliamentary elections. She was pronounced dead at 6:16 p.m. local time at Rawalpindi General Hospital.

Conflicting news stories led to a confusion regarding whether she suffered from gunshot wounds or received her wounds due to shrapnel. AFP quoted Javed Cheema as saying she may have been killed by pellets packed into the suicide bomber's vest. However, the AP quoted a PPP security adviser as saying she was shot in the neck and chest as she got into her vehicle, before the explosion.

Early reports from the hospital stated that Bhutto had a bullet in the back of the neck that damaged her spinal cord before exiting from the side of her head. Another bullet pierced the back of her shoulder and came out through her chest. Bhutto was given an open heart massage, but the main cause of death was damage to her spinal cord.

No official announcement has yet been made. No claims of responsibility were initially reported.

The PPP's Makhdoom Amin Fahim stated that Bhutto

could have survived the blast if she had not stood up in her vehicle. Fahim was sitting in the back seat when she was attacked. She was shot when she stood up by her vehicle's door.

Some news reports include video purported to be Bhutto's departure from the rally, already secured in her bulletproof Toyota Mega Cruiser.

A leading Pakistan newspaper outlined the events of the shooting as follows:

- Bhutto was leaving Liaquat Bagh after addressing the rally when her vehicle, a Black Lexus bulletproof vehicle, stopped near the venue's gate where PPP workers were shouting party slogans.
- Bhutto popped out through the sunroof of her vehicle to respond to her supporters' slogans when a motorcyclist opened Kalashnikov AK-47 gun fire on her.
- Bhutto then fell inside her vehicle after receiving bullet injuries to her head and neck.

Video shows the last moments of the former Prime Minister of Pakistan. Video from the scene also shows several people being loaded into ambulances. There were quite a few cameras rolling, but as of yet, no video has been shown of the actual shooting.

Pakistan Reaction

After the assassination of Bhutto, and in particular the announcement by the PPP spokesman to the press, there were a number of riots resulting in 16 deaths, in which 3 were Police Officers. Around 100 cars were burnt, and angry and upset supporters of Bhutto threw rocks outside the hospital where she was being held.

International Reaction

Main article: *International reaction to the Benazir Bhutto assassination*

The United Nations Security Council met in an emergency session, and subsequently stated that it "unanimously condemned" the assassination. White House spokesman Scott Stanzel condemned "the acts of violence" in the assassination. United States President George W. Bush called it a "cowardly act by murderous extremists" and said the "criminals" responsible "must be brought to justice".

British Prime Minister Gordon Brown condemned the acts saying that it was "a sad day for democracy" and "a tragic hour for Pakistan".

Australian Prime Minster Kevin Rudd joined condemnation of the act, describing it as an "evil" and "cowardly attack". He also said "Australia condemns unequivocally the assassination of Benazir Bhutto, this is an attack on the democracy of Pakistan, this is an attack on the stability of Pakistan, this is an attack on the forces for moderation in Pakistan."

Russian president Vladimir Putin condemned the killing as a "barbarous act of terrorism". Russian Foreign Ministry spokesman Mikhail Kamynin said "We firmly condemn this terrorist act, we express our condolences to Benazir Bhutto's relatives and loved ones, and we hope that the Pakistani leadership will manage to take necessary steps to ensure stability in the country".

The Prime Minister of neighbouring India, Dr. Manmohan Singh, expressed deep shock at the assassination of Benazir Bhutto. Dr Singh stated, "The manner of her going is a reminder of the common dangers that our region faces from cowardly acts of terrorism and of the need to eradicate this dangerous threat." The President of the ruling Indian National Congress, Sonia Gandhi, widow of former Indian Prime Minister Rajiv Gandhi, expressed condolences stating, "This reprehensible act deserves to be strongly condemned by all those who believe in freedom of expression and democratic values".

Stephen Harper, Prime Minister of Canada, said "We condemn this attack in the strongest possible terms — this was an abhorrent act of terror and we hope [that] the government of Pakistan will act and bring the perpetrators to justice. This cannot be allowed to permit any delay in the return of Pakistan to full democracy—something the people of Pakistan have been waiting for for far too long."

Dora Bakoyannis, Foreign Affairs Minister of Greece, speaking on behalf of the government of Prime Minister Kostas Karamanlis, said that "Greece condemns the terrorist attack in the most categorical way that, just two weeks ahead of the Parliamentary elections in Pakistan, has led to this tragic loss. We are watching the events with great concern, at the same time expressing the wish and the hope that this country will follow the path towards the construction of a democratic regime. This will also constitute the sole vindication of the tragic sacrifice of Benazir Bhutto."

Benazir Bhutto's Books

- Benazir Bhutto, (1983), Pakistan: The gathering storm, Vikas Pub. House, ISBN 0706924959
- Benazir Bhutto (1989). Daughter of the East. Hamish Hamilton. ISBN 0-241-12398-4.

Daughter of the East was also released as:

- Benazir Bhutto (1989). Daughter of Destiny: An Autobiography. Simon & Schuster. ISBN 0-671-66983-4.

Books About Benazir Bhutto

- W.F. Pepper, (1983), Benazir Bhutto, WF Pepper, ISBN 0946781001
- Rafiq Zakaria (1990). The Trial of Benazir. Sangam Books. ISBN 0-861-32265-7.
- Katherine M. Doherty, Caraig A. Doherty , (1990), Benazir Bhutto (Impact Biographies Series), Franklin Watts, ISBN 0531109364
- Rafiq Zakaria, (1991), The Trial of Benazir Bhutto:

An Insight into the Status of Women in Islam, Eureka Pubns, ISBN 9679783200

- Diane Sansevere-Dreher, (1991), Benazir Bhutto (Changing Our World Series), Bantam Books (Mm), ISBN 0553158570
- Christina Lamb, (1992), Waiting for Allah, Penguin Books Ltd, ISBN 0140143343
- M FATHERS, (1992), Biography of Benazir Bhutto, W.H. Allen/Virgin Books, ISBN 024554965X
- Elizabeth Bouchard, (1994), Benazir Bhutto: Prime Minister (Library of Famous Women), Blackbirch Pr Inc, ISBN 1567110274
- Iqbal Akhund, (2000), Trial and Error: The Advent and Eclipse of Benazir Bhutto, OUP Pakistan, ISBN 0195791606
- Libby Hughes, (2000), Benazir Bhutto: From Prison to Prime Minister, Backinprint.Com, ISBN 0595003885
- Iqbal Akhund, (2002), Benazir Hukoomat: Phela Daur, Kia Khoya, Kia Paya?, OUP Pakistan, ISBN 0195794214
- Mercedes Anderson, (2004), Benazir Bhutto (Women in Politics), Chelsea House Publishers, ISBN 0791077322
- Mary Englar, (2007), Benazir Bhutto: Pakistani Prime Minister and Activist, Compass Point Books, ISBN 0756517982
- Ayesha Siddiqa Agha, (2007), Military Inc.: Inside Pakistan's Military Economy, Pluto Press, ISBN 0745325459

Appendix I

Nov. 15, 2006—Age has scarcely mellowed Benazir Bhutto. At 53, Pakistan's two-time former prime minister has lost none of the fighting spirit that made her the first woman to be elected leader of a modern Muslim nation nearly two decades ago, when she was only 35. Recently she publicly joined forces with her former political nemesis (and now fellow exile) Nawaz Sharif, renouncing their past feuds and demanding restoration of democracy in Pakistan. Their pact was yet another headache for the country's military leader, Gen. Pervez Musharraf, who already faces a full share of problems in both embattled Kashmir and on the Afghan border, where Osama bin Laden and other Al Qaeda leaders are believed to be hiding. Bhutto recently traveled to New York to lecture at the Oxonian Society and announce her hope of running for prime minister in 2007. She spoke with NEWSWEEK's Karen Fragala Smith about her views on the Taliban, women's rights and the corruption allegations that plagued her political career.

NEWSWEEK: Why Hasn't Osama Bin Laden Been Found?

Benazir Bhutto: I believe that elements of the [Pakistani] military security apparatus have a lot of sympathy for bin

Laden. General Musharraf is relying on the [military] to find bin Laden, and it's simply not going to happen. What we really need is a change, and I believe that change has to come by going to the civilian option.

How would you Rate General Musharraf's Performance as a Partner to the United States in the Bush Administration's Fight Against Terror?

I think General Musharraf took the right decision following the events of 9/11 to stand with the international community to fight terrorism. But I question how effective he has been in eliminating terrorism. There is a lack of implementation of his decisions in many parts of the country, and we have seen in [recent] years how the Taliban have reorganized themselves, and their goal is to take over Afghanistan once again. The religious parties have gained strength within Pakistan and today control of two of our most important provinces that border Afghanistan. Militant groups that were [once] banned—who were attacking New Delhi, Bombay—are re-emerging and hold peace between India and Pakistan hostage. When I look at the rise of the religious parties, the reorganization of the Taliban and the persistence of the militant groups, I worry for Pakistan's future.

Is it True that you Initially Supported the Taliban when they First Formed in Afghanistan?

When the Taliban first emerged, the United States, Pakistan and many other countries saw them as a force for peace, but soon we became disillusioned. There's a difference between Taliban with Al Qaeda and Taliban without Al Qaeda. When the first Taliban emerged, there was no Al Qaeda. They were there as Afghans trying to be a political force within Afghanistan. After the overthrow of my government in 1996, they allowed Al Qaeda to set up training camps. At that time, I was leader of the opposition in the Pakistani Parliament, and I called upon the government to issue an ultimatum to the Taliban that unless they evicted

Al Qaeda, Pakistan would break relations with them. Unfortunately, my calls fell on deaf ears.

Describe your New Alliance with Former Political Rival Nawaz Sharif. What are your Intentions Going Forward?

I traveled to Saudi Arabia last year to meet with Mr. Sharif. I told him that [people] inside and outside Pakistan are concerned that both of us spend so much time fighting each other [and] that if democracy was restored, we might have another round of senseless political battles. We needed to send a signal that we've learned our lessons and that next time it will be different. We came up with a "Charter of Democracy" [which is] aimed at creating a political system of checks and balances. In Pakistan, politics is a zero-sum game, but we believe that there should be a place within the system for divergent political views. A democratic society will also create tolerance among the young people in Pakistan who are confused by conflicting messages. On the one hand, they hear about the beauty of an accountable, transparent governance system that empowers ordinary people. But their reality is that power flows from the gun. We need to reverse the culture of violence and replace it with a culture of law and tolerance.

Pakistan Currently has term Limits that Would Keep you from Returning to Office as Prime Minister. Would you Consider Running in Some other Capacity?

In the immediate future, my party and the alliance with Mr. Sharif are both looking to put an end to the term limits. We feel that it should be left to the people of Pakistan. It's not like America, where a president is elected and he completes [one or] two terms. Our terms are interrupted, so they don't really qualify in the American sense of two terms. I am planning to go back to Pakistan to help my party in the next general elections. If that limitation is lifted, I'll run for prime minister.

Your Administration was Plagued by Corruption Charges

The allegations have been made to destroy my reputation. Despite the rules being stacked against me, none of the courts were able to convict me. I have always proclaimed my innocence, my husband has proclaimed his, and neither of us have been convicted, nor has any other member of my family. These corruption charges have been made to tarnish my image and deny Pakistan a democratic alternative. Since 1950, corruption charges have been made against every civilian prime minister—I believe it's to divert attention from the institutionalized corruption of the military.

What it your View on India-Pakistan Relations?

Irrespective of the differences on Kashmir, India and Pakistan have to move forward. One of the key ways that we can move forward is by copying Europe's example. Europe was torn apart by war until it decided to build a common market. I've spoken to Indian leaders on this, and within Pakistan and India there's an emerging consensus that while we have differences, these differences should not stop us from economic development and cooperation in terms of trade and travel. But obviously we need safe borders. While militants hold guns in their hands and disturb the peace, it's very difficult to get safe and open borders. Attacking militancy is very important, not only vis-à-vis Afghanistan, but also vis-à-vis India.

What do you think of the Current State of Women's Rights in Pakistan?

There's a very big debate on the role of women in the Muslim world. Some claim that women must be kept behind closed doors, but I argue that Islam came to emancipate women, not to repress them. The time has come when we within the Muslim world need to realize that each of us has a right to interpret religion as we wish, and we do not need clerics or the state to tell us how to worship.

What is your Perspective?

When I was first elected prime minister of Pakistan, a leading Saudi cleric said that it was un-Islamic. At the same time, the religious leaders from Yemen, Cairo and Syria all came out in support of a woman leading an Islamic nation. [There is] tremendous debate and discussion between those who would take us to the past, and those who look to the future.

Appendix II

Speech by Leader of Opposition—Benazir Bhutto Chairperson, Pakistan Peoples Party. First Indo-Pak Parliamentarians Conference Held at Islamabad on February 13, 1999

Fellow Parliamentarians

We meet at a time of hope, but also a time of despair. A time of opportunity, but also a time of peril. A time of change, but still a time of intractability.

Ladies and Gentlemen

South Asia has been far too long a region teetering on the edge of catastrophe.

For fifty years, we have been at each other's throats. We have fought four wars, and the last war dismembered my nation. Our troops, as we speak, fire at each other in the frozen wasteland called Siachen, which has become a metaphor for the senselessness that we have allowed to continue for half a century.

With the newly awakened nuclear capabilities of India and Pakistan, and what appears to be a deployment race well underway, we can ill-afford the luxury of ignoring the roots of our deepdistrust towards each other.

It is conventional wisdom that the roots of the Indo-Pak conflict, or more specifically, the enmity Muslims and Hindus are centuries old.

That is a strange notion.

For as many years that India and Pakistan have been at war, for many more centuries our cultures have lived in peaceful co-existence.

Our cultures were, and still are, necessary threads weaving the unique and vibrant cloth called South Asia.

Ladies and Gentlemen

National and world politics in the first half of the 20th Century was driven by geo-strategic considerations, military-territorial considerations. The great empires of the Romans, Arabs, and the British rose on territorial conquest fueled by military strength. Fantastic economical-rewards awaited victorious conquerors in the form of booty, cheep labour and captive markets. The European Colonialism was rooted in this psychology spread over thousands of years. It concluded when the Yalta Agreement was signed between the Big Three. The Cold War era then dawned. However the collapse of the Soviet Union, brought a fundamentally new global system.

It is exciting living at a time of dramatic change in history where military-territorial supremacy dissipates as the era of economic-technological supremacy dawns.

New World Order

History springs from one side of the pendulum to another. With the end of the Cold War, we are back to the world where global politics was driven by economic considerations, where markets are the yardstick by which the power, size and influence of Nations will be judged.

Will we, the people of South Asia, be prisoners of the past or will we be able to rise to a magnificent future?

The collapse of military-territorial superpower, the Soviet Union the rise of Germany, Japan, (South Korea Taiwan, Singapore) sent a powerful message to our generation. Brute military/territorial strength alone (like the Soviet Union) could not save it from disintegration and economic collapse. Germany, Japan and the NIC's rose without military-territorial strength to become economic superpowers. We are eye-witnesses to a New World Order based upon free commerce and trade. A nation's success is measured by its ability to develop products, ideas to sell in the global marketplace, which is open to all. It is based on the quality of goods and services and global demand-supply factors. Suddenly it is possible for tiny Singapore, with a tiny territorial and population base, a quarter of Karachi or Bombay, and a virtually non-existent military base, to become an economic giant, equal to the First World Countries in the quality of life it affords to its citizens.

Rules of the Game

The new rules of the game are that a nation upholds the principles of democracy, the rule of law, guarantees basic freedom and liberties to its citizens, allows free trade and a market driven economy with minimal state intervention, with a policy of non-intervention and mutual respect in inter-state relations. The concern of the state in inter-state relations is also driven by considerations of trade and commerce (again following the Japanese model), rather than by military-territorial considerations.

A nation which lives in the past, bases its thinking on the old paradigm of military-territorial strength, perishes in the New World Order and is treated as a pariah state (e.g. Russia, Yugoslavia, and most recently Iraq).

The success of a Nation, as we head towards a new century, a new millenium, is based upon the level of exports, hard currency reserves, its per capita GNP, and certainly not its territory, military strength, or population base. The pace in the race for economic success has become so competitive, that even First World former superpower nations such as Britain, France and Germany, felt unable to compete individually with today's economic giants, the U.S. and Japan.

The GNP of America is (US$ 8 trillion) and of Japan (US$ 5 trillion). Only after combining the 10 'First World' European economies, the combined EC GNP can compete (at US$ 7 trillion).

The desire for the creation of 'super-economic zones' like the EC, was driven by Britain, France and Germany seeking to effectively compete economically with the economic superpowers namely the United States and Japan. The US, in turn rushed to form NAFTA and APEC as an economic reply to the EC.

All this is accomplished, without a single bullet being fired, with no military adventures or conquests, and yet huge territories, nations and populations peacefully agreed to redefine their economic borders, and to co-exist with each other in the better interests of their future well being. The EC's formation is truly a model case of the new paradigm, where economically we enter an increasingly Borderless World while maintaining our national 'sovereignty'. The EC members states 'pooled' their economic sovereignty in creating a free trade zone and a common currency, thus submerging their narrow national interests for the greater good of the whole European Community. Meanwhile, at the other extreme, a closed nation, closed by sanctions or voluntarily, such as Libya, Iran, Iraq, Afghanistan, Somalia and Sudan suffered economically even when they had huge oil reserves and a tiny population.

Ladies and Gentlemen

If we close our borders and live in the past, our region risks suffering a similar fate to the Soviet Union, Yugoslavia and other such countries.

The Population Bomb

Our two nations are now home to nearly one-fifth of the total human population. The United Nations currently estimates the entire human population to be just shy of six billion people.

Given current rates of population growth, by the year 2015, our two nations combined population will surpass the population of China.

As our populations grow, so too must our capacity to manage precious natural resources.

The path to resolving our conflict lies within these unsettling figures and how we address the very real daily problems of population growth, economic opportunity, healthcare, education and stewardship of our environment.

South Asia—A House Divided

But our conflict also reflects dynamics akin to a large and unruly family. In the final analysis, South Asia is a house, but a house divided.

The history of humankind clearly shows that brothers can have the greatest love for each other, but are also capable of the most venomous hatred and spite.

So it is in the Middle East between the Jews and the Arabs.

Sc it is in Ireland between the Catholics and the Protestants.

So it is in the former Yugoslavia between the Muslims and the Serbs.

So it is in the horn of Africa between the Ethiopians and the Eritreans.

Within our South Asian house, we are no different. We are warring South Asian brothers and sisters.

Personally, both my grand parents lived in the area around present Mumbai (or Bombay). Our ancestral homes remain there today. In the registers of Ajmer Sharif and Hazrat Nizamuddin Auliya, you can see the signatures of my ancestors.

Indo-Pak enmity denied me the opportunity to see my grand parents home, to offer prayers at grandmother's grave, or my aunt Benazir after whom I am named or to take my children to a place that is a part of their history.

Will I be able to do so? Will our generation have the chance to build peace or will we become another Soviet Union, with the largest land mass territory in the world, encompassing two continents, an advanced space programme, enough nuclear warheads and ballistic missiles to destroy the whole world, and a 'superpower' status, ultimately ending up having to beg for food from the EC to feed its population? Ultimately having to ask (relatively) 'tiny' Japan, with no military might, for economic aid?

Ladies and Gentlemen

This is a turning point in history, a different place from 50 years ago. We can strut around the stage pretending we are great powers in the world. Reality tells us that the Russian giant nation is considered an economic minnow today, with even tiny Singapore better off than Russia. 'Giant' India or Pakistan, with all our nuclear bravado, need to face the reality that we are economic pygmies on the world stage, and have a population base of 1.3 billion of the world's poorest people, with the worst standard of living.

Once we understand these objective facts, we can address the problem and find the solutions.

Foreign Policy

Ladies and Gentlemen—In this final year of the second millennium, it is time not only to take stock but to take action, not only to plan for dialogue but to engage in dialogue, not only to talk peace but to make peace?

Could there be any more fitting denouement to the

second millennium than a peaceful resolution to the Indo-Pakistan dispute? I think not.

But if we are to proceed, it will take courage and leadership on behalf of our governments. For, in the words of the philosopher Spinoza, "peace is not mere absence of war, but is a virtue that springs from force of character."

The Nuclear Crisis

We are today in perhaps the most unsettling and dangerous situation since partition itself: a fullblown nuclear race.

I am convinced that none of us know the true horrors of these weapons, nor the devastation nuclear weapons can inflict upon our people when used.

None of us have truly comprehended the dire consequences of a nuclear and ballistic arms race in our land.

With our close knit ecological systems, weather patterns, and dense populations, one nuclear explosion on either side of the border would have the most tragic of consequences for all.

Entering the nuclear arena requires a wisdom and a patience from leaders that, to date, none of us have shown much of.

I admit, I too, in my two terms followed the path of hawkishness.

But that was before India and Pakistan shook the World with their nuclear blasts and brought forward many questions specifically on these weapons of mass destruction. I ask our current leaders:

> Do we have adequate controls over these dangerous weapons?
>
> Have we built clear-cut lines of communications between those who watch these weapons, and those who would decide for their use?

In this new nuclear era, we, Pakistan and India, no longer have the luxury to ignore our suspicions, our mistrust and our foreign policy misadventures.

Both of our nations must step forward cognizant of our political realities.

Both of our nations must step forward, understanding the threat to our people, our region, and the entire world, and declare South Asia a nuclear free and missile free zone.

Today I call upon India and Pakistan to jointly or singly:

1. adhere quickly to the CTBT Treaty
2. a moratorium on fissile material production
3. resist the development, flight testing and storage of ballistic weapons;
4. strengthen export control on nuclear technology

Ladies and Gentlemen

We must step forth and together change the direction of history

On Kashmir

Ladies and Gentlemen

All of our problems, all of our disputes, all of our disagreements can be resolved quickly to mutual satisfaction if we address the question of Jammu and Kashmir.

Yes I know that some in India say this is an internal matter that Kashmir is as much a part of India as Texas is of the United States.

I have heard this before. In fact, I have heard it all my life. And I know better. The issue of Jammu and Kashmir is a problem that has brought us to war before and could very well bring us to war again, this time with the most catastrophic consequences.

In India, extremists say never, no compromise.

In Pakistan, extremists say never, no compromise.

The stakes, my friends, are much too high to let our policy be driven by our political margins. It is time that our policy be driven by reason, and by our commitment to our children's future.

There must be a resolution of the Jammu-Kashmir problem that accounts for the political sensitivities and political desires of the people of that princely state. It is not useful to hear about what a Maharaja did fifty years ago, or where an army attacked, or another army counterattacked.

The fact remains that Jammu and Kashmir is a largely Muslim state, between two nations that were created in a religious partition.

The fact remains that the people of Jammu and Kashmir are politically alienated and disaffected.

The fact remains that an intifida has raged on the ground, and continues as we speak.

The fact remains that Jammu and Kashmir is the densest and largest militarily occupied territory on earth.

And the fact remains that over fifty thousand people have been killed, thousands of women raped, thousands of children kidnapped never to be seen again, scores of villages wiped from the face of the earth.

It is a record that cannot make you proud, and a record that causes us the greatest pain.

No process leading to the fair and equitable resolution of the fifty-year Kashmir conflict can move forward, however, without concrete steps by both Pakistan and India.

The Simla Agreement recognizes this.

On India's part, there are a number of confidence-building measures that could be taken immediately, including:

- A dramatic reduction of the nearly 600,000 troops now stationed in Kashmir.

- Ceasing all forms of torture, intimidation and extra-judicial killings.
- Opening Jammu-Kashmir to monitoring by international human rights groups.

Ultimately we would like to see India begin dialogue with the All Parties Hurriyat Conference (APHC). Likewise, for my part, I will vigorously pursue the following initiatives in Pakistan:

1. Dialogue with India for open borders between Azad Kashmir and Jammu and Kashmir as a prelude to open borders between all of South Asia.
2. Talks for mutual Arms reduction and redeployment of Forces.

I recall that after the end of the Second World War, President Harry Truman faced a dilemma. Europe was in physical and economic shambles. The Soviet Union had engulfed eastern and central Europe and threatened Greece, Turkey, Italy, even France. Obviously, the burden was on the United States to lead in the economic reconstruction of Europe and the political and military containment of communism.

But the American people would have no part of it. Their sons and daughters had spent four years saving Europe, and the American people had had enough. They wanted to return home, build their houses, have their children, and raise their families. They wanted to turn inward.

But Harry Truman was a leader. Despite public opinion polls that showed only 15% support for a massive U.S. engagement in Europe, he created the Marshall Plan and the NATO alliance, and then went out to his people and day by day, month by month, sold the necessity to a skeptical electorate.

He convinced them. He convinced a Congress controlled by the opposition, and he ultimately was re-elected. And the programs that he initiated structured foreign policy for forty years, ultimately resulting in the destruction of the Berlin Wall and the triumph of democracy and the free market.

Why do I relate these points of history, now fifty years later? Because, ladies and gentlemen, it is this kind of foresight and courage which is required now, by leaders in both Pakistan and India, to begin a process of constructive dialogue and conflict resolution and hopefully consensus building. Extremists on both sides of our border might resist, but the masses of our people are looking for compromise. Our people want peace even if they cheer and scream when they are egged on by demagogues with the rhetoric of war.

So let us begin.

I recall quite vividly that the problems of the Middle East were viewed as intractable, unsolvable by men and women of less than grand vision, until Anwar Sadaat broke open the debate by bold action, and began a process that is still unfolding. Like in the dispute between India and Pakistan, the dispute between the Israelis and the Arab nations was manageable and addressable when, and only when, the core issue-the issue of the political rights of the people of Palestine—was successfully addressed. And President Sadaat and Prime Minister Begin won the Nobel Prize for Peace.

I recall vividly that the problems of Northern Ireland were viewed as intractable and irreconcilable by men and women of limited vision, until John Hume, David Trimble, Bill Clinton and George Mitchell restructured the debate, resulting in the extraordinary Good Friday peace treaty which we all pray, Inshallah, will lead to a final peace on that troubled, divided island. And the two men who risked the most, and fought the hardest—Mr. Hume and Mr. Trimble—won the Nobel Prize for Peace.

I recall vividly that few on earth ever thought we would live to see the day that South Africa would flourish under democracy, and the dreaded cancer of apartheid would be radiated from the body politic. But justice prevailed, and leaders with political vision and courage prevailed. And Nelson Mandela became the President of a United South Africa, a black and white South Africa. And the two leaders who made that possible, President Mandela and President DeKlerk, won the Nobel Prize for Peace.

Ladies and gentlemen, in Oslo, there is another set of Nobel Prizes that wait to be awarded to people of courage, to true leaders. They are reserved for leaders of peace in India and Pakistan.

Prime Minister Rajiv Gandhi and I took significant steps to promote peace between 1988-90:

1. We signed non-attack on each other's nuclear facilities
2. We had a defense Secretaries agreement for a settlement in Siachin
3. We expanded the trade list between our two countries.
4. We exchanged delegations on the Wullar Barrage issue.
5. We explored the Sir Creek matter.

But then he called for elections and death took him away before he could return to office.

It was at that time—December 1988—that the other SAARC countries accepted the proposals of a world's youngest elected chief executive to:

a) Declare 1989 the year of the Girl child;

b) Allow Parliamentarians and Judges to visit SAARC countries on a SAARC Pass which required no visa;

c) Allow for a common SAARC pre-stamped Mailing System so that families could remain easily in touch with each other.

It is time to pick up the threads again

A Shared Past to Build the Future

The South Asian region encompassing Pakistan, India, Bangladesh, Nepal and Sri Lanka, has a common and shared history. We speak the same language. Our colour is the same. Our thinking, values, pre-47 history and culture is the same. We have a multi-religious society with Muslims, Hindus, Sikhs, Christians, Parsees, Buddhists, and others. Each in our countries believe in freedom of religion, in safety and security resisting outside coercion or intervention. In Dubai, Singapore, or London, a representative sample of the entire gamut of our population and religious spectrum has learnt to co-exist peacefully. The post nuclear era in the sub-continent calls upon us to define a new paradigm and a new set of rules for the game in South Asia.

New Rules for South Asia

The essence of the new paradigm for South Asia is to organize government and economic affairs in a manner which delivers the maximum progress to the regional population in the shortest period of time, with the least wastage in resources.

The fastest route to economic development and growth for our suffering people is the generation of critical economic mass through formation of larger ' economic free zones'. Unless South Asia pulls itself out of the quagmire of poverty, prejudice and the past to change, our people will remain slaves in the global economy carrying out menial low paying tasks for the rich citizens of the First World. Our nations are faced with the choice: either continue as warring sovereign states who continue to carry the "Third World" label for the next 100 years, or pool our resources to create an Asian economic powerhouse comparable to the EC. Should we embark upon the logical route (not necessarily a forgone conclusion given our history of taking the path of 'greatest' resistance), and decide on pooling economic sovereignty and creating an EC type South Asian economic free zone, then we need to ask: what obvious partners are available for India and Pakistan?

An Asian Free Zone

The disparities in per capita income between India and Asean are too great. China and India are different in per capita income, in GNP, and at different stages of their economic evolution cycles. There are differences too in the economic and legal systems (Capitalists/Communists). Pakistan, Bangladesh, Sri Lanka, and Nepal are the obvious candidates for India as partners, for these countries:

(1) have similar per capita income,

(2) all are in similar stages of their economic development life cycles,

(3) all share a common legal system based on English Law,

(4) all have free market based economies,

(5) all share English as a common language for Government and business,

(6) all share a common history and culture.

From Pakistan's perspective, the Gulf Arab States (GCC) are a far cry as they yet have to partner with common Arab countries such as Egypt and Syria. ECO (and RCD before that) has yet to take off due to the different historical backgrounds, per capita incomes, and different stages of economic development (with Turkey wooing the EC). Afghanistan and CIS States, are behind Pakistan in their growth cycles, with a host of other problems such as language, legal systems, per capita income, and the fact that the CIS States are bound together under the Russian CIS confederation system. Pakistan cannot economically integrate with China for the same reasons as India. Therefore for Pakistan too the logical choice for a long term EC style partnership, are the South Asian nations.

Had the South Asian nations been Muslim countries,

our partnership would have taken place long ago. Yet, if religion was the criteria which bound States together, then Bangladesh would still be East Pakistan and Pakistan would be free of provincialism, sectarianism, and every other kind of 'ism'.

Based on this analysis my recommendation is that in Phase I, the South Asian nations agree to form a free economic zone. This zone could comprise all SAARC countries, plus Iran (or even all the ECO States if they are willing to join). Phase I can conclude in a decade allowing the founding members to reach a critical phase in their economic development and in their per capita income. In Phase II, China could be included in the Free Zone.

This is a vision of an Asian Free Zone which by 2010 can be in existence with 2.5 to 3 billion people, and with a GNP of US$ 7 trillion (based upon 1998 'Purchasing Power Parity'). Of this GNP, roughly 2/3 would be China, and 1/3 SAARC States. Our Asian Free Zone could then be at the same level, in GNP terms, as EC, US or Japan.

With roughly 50% of the World's population located in the Asian Zone, this zone in terms of an economic market would have the greatest influence, voice and clout in the 21st Century.

As one of America's Senators, Barbara Mikulski, recently said, "demography is destiny." And if demography is destiny, the future belongs to Asia.

In terms of demographics, in terms of production, in terms of consumption, in terms of markets, in terms of an expanding capital intensive middle class, the Asian continent will set the tone, set the pace, and dominate the economic and geopolitical trends of the coming era.

The states of the 'Asian Free Zone' would be independent sovereign nations on the pattern of the EC sharing (1) a free economic trade zone (2) a common Central Bank with a common trading currency (3) a common security policy and ultimately (4) a common revolving Presidency and

Parliament (like the EC Presidency and Parliament) Even the smallest member state, such as Sri Lanka through this cooperation could have a chance to be the President of the 'superpower' Asian Zone.

Principles of the Asian free Zone

Let's see what is considered "In" and what "Out" in the proposed Asian Free Zone:

IN	*OUT*
-Free trade	-Protected and closed markets
-Democratic systems down to provincial rights rights	-Centralized govt., with limited province/state level with maximum provincial and local
-Free movement of people	-Closed borders
-Rule of law, guarantee of	-Authoritarianism civil liberties
-Respect of all religions, castes,	-Old religious hatreds creeds
-State is servant and economic	-State has a 'raja' mentality facilitator
-State spends budget on health, education, etc	-State spends budget on defense
-Close cordial & friendly state	-Cold war in South Asia relations
-State creates environment for a new NIC	-State creates environment for a new Russia
-Ultimately aim for the European state model of a suprastructure of independent states	-Aim for the Soviet State model domination and hegemony by the Centre

The Future

Ladies & Gentlemen—We are the ones who have to reach to transform our people's future in a single generation. South Asia combined with Iran and China can comprise the largest population concentration region in the World with 2.6 billion people, over 50% of the global population. We can choose to become a super economic zone, enjoying a life style similar to the European people or we can cling on to our Third World status and continue to blame "foreign powers" for our miseries.

The choice is in our hands.

Not in the hands of our fathers.

Not in the hands of Nehru, Bhutto, Bandaranaike or Mujeeb.

The choice is not in the hands of the coming generations.

Not in the hands of our children.

Our hands will shape the destiny of South Asia, that course, that history which will flow for the next hundred years.

We are gifted to be at this special time, at this special place, in this special representative capacity as one-century wanes and another dawns. Our thoughts, ideas, and deeds can make the difference.

Let me tell you about my country.

Pakistan has paid a very heavy price in the spin off from the Afghan War. This includes the Klashinikov culture in Karachi, the rapid and alarming rise in the number of drug addicts who are estimated at over four million, the spillover of militants from trainee camps across the border, which has exacerbated tensions with our neighbours and disturbed internal security. Many Pakistanis were amazed to learn when the US Cruise Missiles hit Khost that six of the dead were Pakistanis. According to the UN, when Bahmiyan in North Afghanistan fell, Pakistanis were amongst the prisoners taken. Threats of terrorism and militancy to Pakistan from across the border are real.

Drugs, terrorism, extremism and violence are dangers which call for Pakistanis to put greater attention to what is happening in Afghanistan and could happen in Pakistan.

Let me tell you about our polity.

In Pakistan there are different kinds of political parties.

Some proclaim an Islamic system to win power.

Some claim provincial autonomy/nationalism as the answer.

Others pursue the politics of sectarianism to achieve their goals.

Still others believe the politics of ethnicity will lead to deliverance.

A few without electoral support cling to the notion of climbing into power through a military backed interim government.

The Pakistan Peoples Party believes in the politics of the people. Our goal is the economic emancipation of our people. We want our peoples to have freedom to chose, to practice. They are free to follow any sect, speak any ethnic language, practice their beliefs as they interpret religion. It is not our job.

Our job is to provide freedom and economic emancipation.

Quaid-e-Awam Zulfikar Ali Bhutto saw socialism as the route to economic emancipation in the seventies.

His daughter led the drive for economic emancipation through decentralization, deregulation privatization and free market.

For the coming decade, given the global realities, the path to economic salvation, to economic emancipation, to opportunity, prosperity, dignity, hope and success lies in a free economic zone.

Fellow Parliamentarians—Will we be condemned to the miseries of an unfortunate past or will we demonstrate the courage and conviction to seize a fantastic future?

Will we allow the frenzied calls of fanatics to dictate the agenda or will we allow the cool logic of the information technology world to drive an agenda of change?

Will we choose the path of Satti and Karo Kari or will we break free of outmoded traditions?

Will we torture and suppress our people, in fear, or will we respect people's dignity and self determination, in confidence?

Will we blind ourselves to old battles or see the new ones, the real ones that need to be fought.

My father, whom I loved deeply, was born in the British Raj. He lived through an epoch period of the Second World War, the freedom struggle, the collapse of Colonialism.

As a young student I heard his brilliant address at the United Nations. I heard him say, "Mr. Secretary General, realities change. The reality was that German troops were at the gates of Stalingrad". Realities change. Indeed, realities change.

But I would say definitions change too.

The people of South Asia are an honourable people, a self respecting people. Honour and respect through the centuries have carried different definitions.

There was a time when we honoured the warriors who raped, looted and plundered calling them great Conquerors and Emperors.

Today we honour a Nelson Mandela who makes peace and are appalled by those who rape, plunder and pillage.

There was a time when we honoured a man who look revenge for the murder of his family or tribe. Today we are shocked and punish those who take the law into their own hands.

There was a time when honour demanded that we lock up our wives in women's quarters. Today we consider it barbaric.

Realities change and with them definitions. There is no honour when people commit suicide because they cannot afford to live.

There is no honour when a child is born burdened with its country's debt.

There is no honour when a sniper's bullet kills a father on his way to work destroying a family's joy.

Since the Berlin Wall fell, we have seen the First World move towards larger economic entities. We have seen that mighty armies could not save Communist or Third World Countries from disintegrating into Warlords who dishonored humanity with bloodshed and carnage.

- Warlords ruled and ruined Lebanon at a time
- Warlords ruled and ruined Somalia
- Warlords ruled and ruined Afghanistan
- Warlords ruled and ruined Chechnya, Bosnia, Sudan and parts of Central Asia.
- Armed Mafias rule and ruined parts of Russia.

Mighty armies watched helplessly as warlords or armed Mafias took over.

The IMF and World Bank are not charities to help South Asia survive. They can give us loans for a time to keep us afloat. But if we fail to learn to survive, who will take us to shore.

Ladies and Gentlemen—Honoured Parliamentarians,

Will we learn from the First World Countries with trillion dollars economies or will we condemn the coming generations to warlords and armed Mafias who will fight and kill.

The unipolar world has no reason to act as a police man unless its vital interests are involved. The carnage in Bosnia continued for years in the heart of Europe. The killing in Kosovo has yet to push the world into action.

You and I, we, the people, we the elected representatives have to police our own world by ensuring democracy, human rights, good governance and creating a macro-economic frame work where our people can compete successfully and where South Asia can go on to make its mark in a new century, a new millenium.

Parliamentarians

In just over 300 days, we will witness, only for the third time in recorded history, the turning of the millenium.

Where, and what, will we be when the year 2000 lights up the night's sky?

Will we be liberated to the endless possibilities of a remarkable new future?

Ladies and Gentlemen

I see a 21st Century of miraculous opportunity.

I see a 21st Century where temples are not brunt nor mosques razed to the ground.

I see a 21st Century where Human Rights are universal and self-determination reigns supreme.

I see a 21st Century where civil dialogue replaces the rhetoric of war and consensus guides the South Asian debate.

I see a 21st Century where people's trust in government is restored, and government gets on with alleviating the miseries and hardships of the people.

I see a 21st Century where every child is planned , wanted, nurtured and supported.

I see a 21st Century of tolerance and pluralism, where religions respect other religions.

I see a 21st Century of equal rights for women and men.

I see a 21st Century where the birth of a girl is welcomed with the same joy as the birth of a boy.

This can be the moment of Change

This can be the moment of Hope

This can be the moment for Leadership

The stakes will never be more important.

The risks never more dangerous.

In the words of the UNESCO Constitution, "since wars begin in the minds of men, it is in the minds of the men that defences of peace must be constructed."

Our ancestors watch.

Our children and grand children's future awaits.

And long after we are gone, and the pages of this keynote address has turned first to sepia, and then to dust, let the history books of India and Pakistan declare that, in the last year of second millenium, moderate and reasonable men and women seized the moment, seized the day, and through courage and conviction shaped a permanent peace for generations yet unknown.

That is the 21st Century I see, for my children and for yours.

Thank you Ladies and Gentlemen.

Appendix III

140 KILLED AS 2 BLASTS TARGET BENAZIR

KARACHI: At least 140 people were killed and hundreds injured late on Thursday night as suspected suicide bombers targeted former prime minister Benazir Bhutto on her return from eight years in selfimposed exile.

Two explosions went off a minute apart shortly after midnight near Karsaz close to the vehicle Ms Bhutto was travelling in, at the head of a procession of hundreds of thousands of Pakistan People's Party (PPP) supporters who had flooded the streets of Karachi to welcome the return of their leader.

The attack bore the hallmarks of Al Qaeda and resembled assassination attempts by militants linked to the terrorist network on President General Pervez Musharraf and Prime Minister Shaukat Aziz in recent years. Intelligence reports also warned of threats of suicide attacks against Ms Bhutto by militants linked to Al Qaeda, the Taliban and Baitullah Mehsud, the Sindh home secretary said on Wednesday.

"The blasts hit two police vehicles which were escorting the truck carrying Ms Bhutto. The target was the truck," senior Karachi police official Azhar Farooqui told Reuters.

Benazir safe: Ms Bhutto was leading the procession to Quaid-e-Azam's mausoleum, where she was to give a speech. However, after the two explosions, she was rushed to the safety of Bilawal House.

"Benazir Bhutto was immediately taken to her ancestral Bilawal House after the blast," Interior Ministry spokesman Javed Cheema told AFP. "She's absolutely safe."

Rehman Malik, an aide to Ms Bhutto who was travelling with her on the truck, said the blasts went off while she was resting inside the vehicle.

Rescuers scrambled to drag bodies from the twisted wreckage of blazing vehicles as fires broke out at the site. "More than two dozen vehicles, including police mobile units, were completely shattered," eyewitnesses told newsmen.

Militant threats: Sindh IG Ziaul Hassan told Geo news late last night that militants have threatened more suicide attacks against Ms Bhutto.

"There were two blasts, one on the left side and one on the right side of the procession," Interior Minister Aftab Sherpao said. "It appears these were suicide attacks, but it is not confirmed."

Suicide bombing: SP Raja Umer Khitab told newsmen the first blast was a suicide attack. He said the police had recovered part of a torso wearing a suicide jacket, as well as the head and hands and feet of the suicide bomber.

According to witnesses, the bomber tried to enter the inner security cordon of PPP workers around Ms Bhutto but was stopped, and then he set off the explosion. Witnesses said the second blast originated from a golden-coloured Pajero parked on the road.

Forty dead bodies were taken to the Liaquat National Hospital, 60 to the JPMC, 27 to Civil Hospital, two to AKUH and three to Zubaida Medical Centre, a death toll of 132, hospital officials told Media men.

BB Demands Raemoval of IB Chief

LAHORE: Former prime minister Benazir Bhutto has demanded that the government sack Intelligence Bureau (IB) chief Brig (r) Ijaz Shah, PPP spokesman Senator Farhatullah Babar quoted her as saying after the late night blasts on Thursday in Karachi that killed dozens of people. Ms Bhutto's husband Zardari told Geo TV that he did not think that extremist elements were behind these blasts, adding that some elements within the government, including some ministers, were responsible for the blasts. He said the PPP was a democratic party and was not a threat to jihadi elements. He said some ministers were also on the hit list of jihadi elements. He said he knew some people sitting in the government who could possibly be behind these blasts.

President, PM Slam Karachi Blasts

ISLAMABAD: President General Pervez Musharraf and Prime Minister Shaukat Aziz have condemned explosions that hit the convoy of former premier Benazir Bhutto late on Thursday in Karachi, killing dozens of people. Such acts cannot deter the government from its resolve to combat extremism and terrorism, they said in separate messages. They condoled with bereaved families, and directed the authorities concerned to provide all possible assistance to the injured. "This was an act of terrorism targeting Benazir Bhutto and aimed at sabotaging the democratic process," Interior Minister Aftab Sherpao told AFP. "We suspect these were suicide bombings because any pre-planted or timed device would have been prevented by jammers attached to security vehicles," he added.

US, UN denounce Attacks on Bhutto

WASHINGTON: The United States on Thursday denounced attacks on former premier Benazir Bhutto's convoy and said the blasts would not derail the country's coming elections. United Nations Chief Ban Ki-moon also condemned the bomb attacks. "The United States condemns the violent attack in Pakistan and mourns the loss of innocent life there," White House national security spokesman Gordon Johndroe said after two bombs left many dead and scores of others wounded. "Extremists will not be allowed to stop Pakistanis from selecting their representatives through an open and democratic process," Johndroe said. Also, US State Department Spokesman Tom Casey said in a press statement, "Our prayers are with the victims and their families.

Appendix IV

The Trials of Benazir Bhutto-a Chronology

Former Pakistan prime minister Benazir Bhutto returned to her homeland Thursday after spending eight years in self-imposed exile in London and Dubai.

Former Pakistan prime minister Benazir Bhutto returned to her homeland Thursday after spending eight years in self-imposed exile in London and Dubai.

The following are some of the key events in her career:

April 1979: Benazir Bhutto is imprisoned just before her father, Zulfikar Ali Bhutto, is executed by Gen Zia ul Huq. She is sentenced to five years in jail.

1984: Bhutto allowed to leave for London for health reasons after spending most of her years in prison in solitary confinement. Bhutto reorganises her father's Pakistan People's Party (PPP) in London and takes over its leadership.

April 1986: Bhutto returns from exile in London and holds political rallies, attracting massive crowds.

Dec 6, 1988: Bhutto becomes the first woman prime minister of a Muslim nation after winning parliamentary elections.

Aug 6, 1990: Bhutto government dismissed by President Ghulam Ishaq Khan on grounds of corruption charges against her and husband Asif Zardari. Her political opponent Nawaz Sharif, of the Pakistan Muslim League, is made prime minister.

July 1993: President Ghulam Ishak Khan dismisses Sharif as prime minister, also on grounds of alleged corruption.

Oct 19, 1993: Bhutto takes oath for a second term as prime minister after elections in which no party is a clear winner. She takes the support of smaller parties.

Sep 1996: Murtaza Bhutto, Benazir's younger brother, is shot dead by policemen along with six of his political workers.

Nov 5, 1996: Bhutto government dismissed again—this time by President Farooq Leghari, not only on charges of corruption but also of carrying out staged killings.

Feb 1997: Sharif becomes prime minister again after his PML convincingly wins general elections.

April 14, 1999: Bhutto and Zardari found guilty of corruption charges involving a Swiss company, while she is out of the country. Zardari goes to jail, and Bhutto remains in exile.

May 1999: Pakistani troops and militants occupy positions in the Kargil area of Kashmir. Strains emerge between Sharif and Musharraf after international condemnation led by the US.

Oct 1999: Sharif sacks Musharraf, but the general hits back by leading an army coup against him and taking control of administration.

Aug 2000: Musharraf bars Bhutto and Sharif from active politics.

Dec 2000: Sharif goes into exile.

July 2002: Court sentences Bhutto (in absentia) to three years in prison on corruption charges.

July 2003: A Swiss court convicts Bhutto and Zardari for money laundering. Given jail sentences and fine.

Nov 2003: Sentence overturned by a higher court.

Nov 2004: Zardari released from prison in Pakistan.

Mar 2005: PPP says it is increasing contact with Musharraf.

Oct 5, 2007: Musharraf signs a corruption amnesty against Bhutto.

Oct 6, 2007: Musharraf wins presidential election.

Oct 18, 2007: Bhutto returns to Pakistan from eight years in self-exile.

Nov 15, 2007: Musharraf's five-year presidential term and the term of the sitting parliament expires.

Jan 14, 2008: The latest date for parliamentary elections.

Index

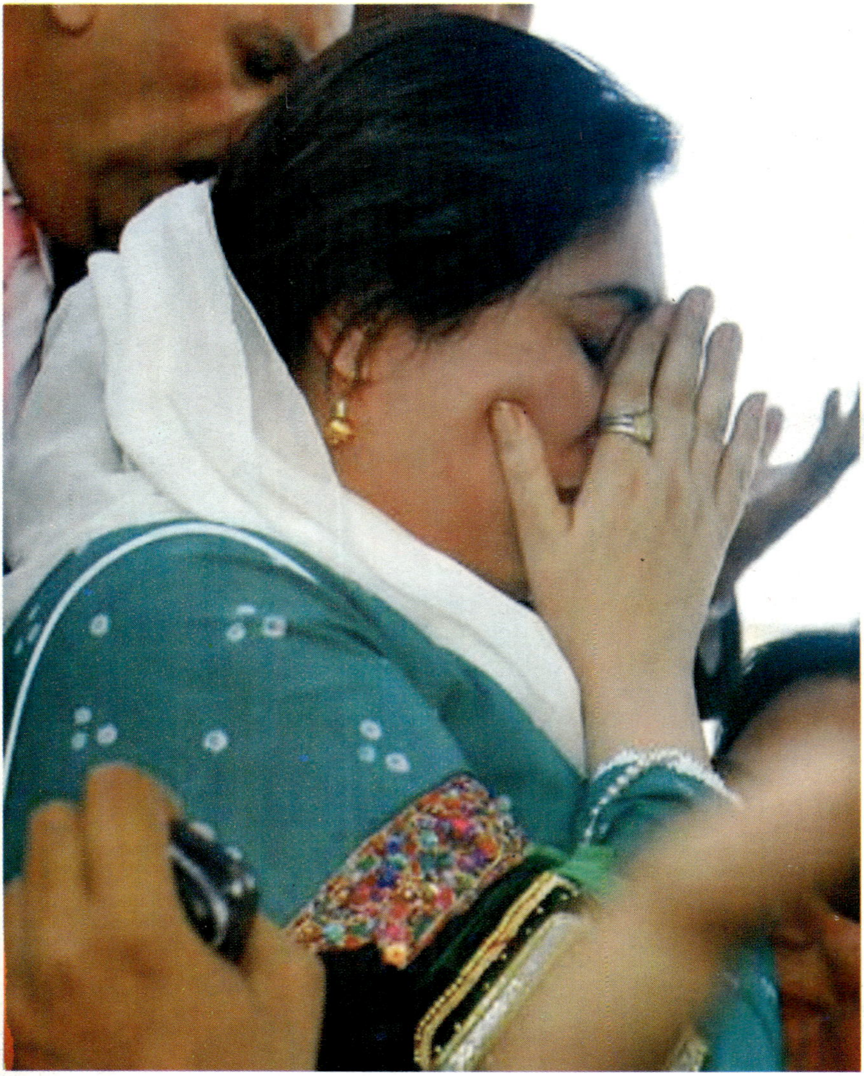